Praise for Michael E. Gerber, Dr. Frank Sovinsky, and *The E-Myth Chiropractor*

This is a must-read for all chiropractors, no matter what age you are or what stage you are at in your career. The book covers many areas of practice. One of the most interesting for me was managing a staff, which the book says is impossible. However, the authors do tell you how to manage the *process*, which is possible. This book will take a real burden off the doctor and let him or her do what he or she does best, which is getting people well.

Arlan W. Fuhr, DC, co-founder and CEO, Activator Methods International

One of my prized possessions is a 1986 first-edition, hardbound copy of *The E-Myth*. Now it is joined by this volume, which successfully adapts the time-tested E-Myth principles for the chiropractor and chiropractic practice. Most chiropractors want a practice, but discover that it is a small business. **Congratulations for providing a roadmap for integrating the Practitioner's Brain with the Business Brain!**

William D. Esteb, Patient Media

I love *The E-Myth Chiropractor!* Michael E. Gerber and Dr. Frank Sovinsky have partnered to share their wisdom in this informative how-to book. **Their wisdom is a blend of intellectual knowledge and life experience, plus reflection on what works. A must-have in every DC's library.** *The E-Myth Chiropractor* holds keys to open the door to success in your practice and fulfillment in your life. All you have to do is open the book, turn the page, read, and apply.

Dr. Liz Anderson-Peacock, BSc, DC, DICCP; CEO, Girls Gals
Gurus Inc.; author, *Pearls of Wisdom: Pure and Powerful*

I just finished reading *The E-Myth Chiropractor*, and the one word that came to my mind was "refreshing." The book is refreshing in the sense that it offers forthright honesty and a consistently ethical approach regarding concepts about the "business of the business," which is developing a successful chiropractic practice. **To any doctor who wants to grow his/her practice from the ground up, this book is the "miracle grow" for your practice.** Throughout the book, in each and every chapter, is a gem of knowledge polished brightly by years of experience and finely tuned with advice that is ethical and relevant. *The E-Myth Chiropractor* is a well-organized guide and a must-read for anyone who wants to begin to work "on" his or her practice.

Louis Sportelli, DC; practitioner

Finally, a book that is full of wisdom and a must-read for all practicing chiropractors. **Do not just recommend this book; buy it and give it to those you care about.**

Bill J. Bonnstetter, founder and chairman of the board, Target Training International and TTI Performance Systems Ltd.; author, *If I Knew Then What I Know Now*

Michael Gerber's *E-Myth* is one of only four books I recommend as required reading. **For those looking to start and build a business of their own, this is the man who has coached more successful entrepreneurs than the next ten gurus combined.**

Timothy Ferris, #1 New York Times best-selling author, *The 4-Hour Workweek*

Everyone needs a mentor, someone who tells it like it is, holds you accountable, and shows you your good, bad, and ugly. For millions of small business owners, Michael Gerber is that person. Let Michael be your mentor and you are in for a kick in the pants, the ride of a lifetime.

John Jantsch, author, *Duct Tape Marketing*

Michael Gerber's strategies in *The E-Myth* were instrumental in building my company from two employees to a global organization; I can't wait to see how applying the strategies from *Awakening the Entrepreneur Within* will affect its growth!

Dr. Ivan Misner, founder and chairman, BNI; author, *Masters of Sales*

Michael Gerber's gift to isolate the issues and present simple, direct, business-changing solutions shines bright with *Awakening the Entrepreneur Within*. **If you're interested in developing an entrepreneurial vision and plan that inspires others to action, buy this book, read it, and apply the processes Gerber brilliantly defines.**

Tim Templeton, author, *The Referral of a Lifetime*

Michael Gerber is a master instructor and a leader's leader. As a combat F15 fighter pilot, I had to navigate complex missions with life-and-death consequences, but until I read *The E-Myth* and met Michael Gerber, my transition to the world of small business was a nightmare with no real flight plan. **The hands-on, practical magic of Michael's turnkey systems magnified by the raw power of his keen insight and wisdom have changed my life forever.**

Steve Olds, CEO, Stratworx.com

Michael Gerber truly, truly understands what it takes to be a successful practicing entrepreneur and business owner. He has demonstrated to me over six years of working with him that for those who stay the course and learn much more than just "how to work on their business and not in it" then they will reap rich rewards. **I finally franchised my business, and the key to unlocking this kind of potential in any business is the teachings of Michael's work.**

Chris Owen, marketing director, Royal Armouries (International) PLC

My wife, Colleen, and I spent twenty-five years flying in the United States Air Force and with commercial airlines. When we changed our career focus and decided to open our own business, we read dozens of books and attended countless seminars. Nothing came close to the quality and precision of the environment that we had lived in for all those years—until we read Michael Gerber's books. His insightful writings finally gave us the flight plan that we had been missing. **We carry copies of his books in our car and share them with other entrepreneurs, because we know that their lives and businesses can be changed in a profound way by the wisdom of Michael Gerber.**

Bill and Colleen Hensley, founders, Hensley Properties Inc.;
authors, *The Pilot-Learning Leadership*

Michael's work has been an inspiration to us. **His books have helped us get free from the out-of-control life that we once had. His no-nonsense approach kept us focused on our ultimate aim rather than day-to-day stresses. He has helped take our business to levels we couldn't have imagined possible.** In the Dreaming Room made us totally re-evaluate how we thought about our business and our life. We have now redesigned our life so we can manifest the dreams we unearthed in Michael's Dreaming Room.

Jo and Steve Davison, founders, The Spinal Health Clinic
Chiropractic Group and www.your-dream-life.com

Rarely—maybe once in a lifetime—is there a message that transforms us, that inspires us to create the vision that describes the grandest version of ourselves, and then act upon it. Several years ago, we heard such a message, Michael Gerber's message. Since then, our journey with Michael has truly awakened the entrepreneur within us! We can't wait to take our lives and the lives of our clients to the next level through this book!

Robert and Susan Clements, principals, E-Myth Iowa

Because of Michael Gerber, I transformed my twenty-four-hour-a-day, seven-day-a-week job (also called a small business) into a multimillion turnkey business. This in turn set the foundation for my worldwide training firm. **I am living my dream because of Michael Gerber.**

Howard Partridge, Phenomenal Products Inc.

Michael Gerber is an outrageous revolutionary who is changing the way the world does business. **He dares you to commit to your grandest dreams and then shows you how to make the impossible a reality. If you let him, this man will change your life.**

Fiona Fallon, founder, Divine and The Bottom Line

Michael Gerber is a genius. Every successful business person I meet has read Michael Gerber, refers to Michael Gerber, and lives by his words. You just can't get enough of Michael Gerber. **He has the innate (and rare) ability to tap into one's soul, look deeply, and tell you what you need to hear. And then, he inspires you, equips you with the tools to get it done.**

Pauline O'Malley, CEO, TheRevenueBuilder

When asked "Who was the most influential person in your life?" I am one of the thousands who don't hesitate to say "Michael E. Gerber." **Michael helped transform me from someone dreaming of retirement to someone dreaming of working until age one hundred.** This awakening is the predictable outcome of anyone reading Michael's new book.

Thomas O. Bardeen

Michael Gerber is an incredible business philosopher, guru, perhaps even a seer. He has an amazing intuition, which allows him to see in an instant what everybody else is missing; he sees opportunity everywhere. **While in the Dreaming Room, Michael gave me the gift of seeing through the eyes of an awakened entrepreneur, and instantly my business changed from a regional success to serving clients on four continents.**

Keith G. Schiehl, president, Rent-a-Geek Computer Services

Michael Gerber is among the very few who truly understand entrepreneurship and small business. While others talk about these topics in the form of theories, methodologies, processes, and so on, Michael goes to the heart of the issues. **Whenever Michael writes about entrepreneurship, soak it in as it is not only good for your business, but great for your soul.** His words will help you to keep your passion and balance while sailing through the uncertain sea of entrepreneurship.

Raymond Yeh, co-author, *The Art of Business*

Michael Gerber's insight, wisdom, caring, and straightforward approach helped me reinvent myself and my business while doubling my revenues in less than one year. Crack open this book and let him do the same for you, too.

Christine Kloser, author, *The Freedom Formula* and *Conscious Entrepreneurs*

Michael Gerber forced me to think big, think real, and gave me the support network to make it happen. A new wave of entrepreneurs is rising, much in thanks to his amazing efforts and very practical approach to doing business.

Christian Kessner, founder, Higher Ground Retreats and Events

Michael's understanding of entrepreneurship and small business management has been a difference maker for countless businesses, including Infusion Software. **His insights into the entrepreneurial process of building a business are a must-read for every small business owner.** The vision, clarity, and leadership that came out of our Dreaming Room experience were just what our company needed to recognize our potential and motivate the whole company to achieve it.

Clate Mask, president and CEO, Infusion Software

Michael Gerber is a truly remarkable man. His steady openness of mind and ability to get to the deeper level continues to be an inspiration and encouragement to me. **He seems to always ask that one question that forces the new perspective to break open and he approaches the new coming method in a fearless way.**

Rabbi Levi Cunin, Chabad of Malibu

The Dreaming Room experience was literally life-changing for us. **Within months, we were able to start our foundation and make several television appearances owing to his teachings.** He has an incredible charisma, which is priceless, but above all Michael Gerber awakens passion from within, enabling you to take action with dramatic results . . . starting today!

Shona and Shaun Carcary, Trinity Property Investments Inc.—Home Vestors franchises

I thought *E-Myth* was an awkward name! What could this book do for me? **But when I finally got to reading it . . . it was what I was looking for all along.** Then, to top it off, I took a twenty-seven-hour trip to San Diego just to attend the Dreaming Room, where Michael touched my heart, my mind, and my soul.

Helmi Natto, president, Eye 2 Eye Optics, Saudi Arabia

I attended In the Dreaming Room and was challenged by Michael Gerber to "Go out and do what's impossible." So I did; **I became an author and international speaker and used Michael's principles to create a world-class company that will change and save lives all over the world.**

Dr. Don Kennedy, MBA; author, *5 AM & Already Behind,* www.bahbits.com

I went to the Dreaming Room to have Michael Gerber fix my business. He talked about Dreaming. What was this Dreaming? I was too busy working! Too busy being miserable, angry, frustrated, behind in what I was trying to accomplish. And losing everything I was working for. **Then Michael Gerber woke up the dreamer in me and remade my life and my business.**

Pat Doorn, president, Mountain View Electric Ltd.

Michael Gerber can captivate a room full of entrepreneurs and take them to a place where they can focus on the essentials that are the underpinning of every successful business. He gently leads them from where they are to where they need to be in order to change the world.

Francine Hardaway, CEO, Stealthmode Partners; founder,
the Arizona Entrepreneurship Conferences

The E Myth Chiropractor

Why Most Chiropractic Practices Don't Work and What to Do About It

MICHAEL E. GERBER

FRANK R. SOVINSKY, DC

PRODIGY
BUSINESS BOOKS

Published by
Prodigy Business Books, Inc., Carlsbad, California.

Production Team
Trish Beaulieu, book division manager, Dezign Matters Creative Group, Inc.;
Helen Chang, editor, helenchangwriter.com; Erich Broesel, cover designer,
BroselDesign, Inc.; Nancy Ratkiewich, book production, njr productions;
Jeff Kassebaum, Michael E. Gerber author photographer, Jeff Kassebaum and Co.;
Rod Evans, Dr. Frank Sovinsky co-author photographer, Evan's Photography

For general information on other products and services, please visit the website:
www.michaelegerber.com

ISBN 978-0-9835001-2-4 (pbk)
ISBN 978-0-9835001-3-1 (cloth)
ISBN 978-0-9835542-1-9 (ebk)

Printed in the United States of America

10 9 8 7 6 5 4 3 2 1

To Luz Delia, whose heart expands mine,
whose soul inspires mine,
whose boldness reaches for the stars, thank you,
forever, for being, truly mine…

—Michael E. Gerber

CONTENTS

A WORD ABOUT THIS BOOK

Michael E. Gerber

My first E-Myth book was published in 1985. It was called *The E-Myth: Why Most Small Businesses Don't Work and What to Do About It*. Since that book, and the company I created to provide business development services to its many readers, millions have read *The E-Myth* and the book that followed it, called *The E-Myth Revisited*, and tens of thousands have participated in our E-Myth Mastery programs.

The co-author of this book, Frank Sovinsky, DC, is one of my more enthusiastic readers, and as a direct result of his enthusiasm, his chiropractic practice became one of those clients. He became, over the years, one of my friends.

This book is two things: the product of my lifelong work conceiving, developing, and growing the E-Myth way into a business model that has been applied to every imaginable kind of company in the world, as well as a product of Dr. Frank's extraordinary experience and success applying the E-Myth to the development of his equally extraordinary enterprise, DC Mentors.

So it was that one day, while sitting with my muse, which I think of as my inner voice, and which many who know me think of as "here he goes again!" I thought about the creation of an entire series of E-Myth Expert books. That series, including this book, would be co-authored by experts in every industry who had successfully applied my E-Myth principles to the extreme development of a practice—a very small company—with the intent of growing it nationwide, and even worldwide, which is what Dr. Frank had in mind as he began to discover the almost infinite range of opportunities provided by thinking the E-Myth way.

Upon seeing the possibilities of this new idea, I immediately invited co-authors such as Dr. Frank to join me. They said, "Let's do it!" and so we did.

Welcome to *The E-Myth Chiropractor: Why Most Chiropractic Practices Don't Work and What to Do About It.*

Read it, enjoy it, and let us—Dr. Frank and I—help you apply the E-Myth to the re-creation, development, and extreme growth of your chiropractic practice into an enterprise that you can be justifiably proud of.

To your life, your wisdom, and the life and success of your clients, I wish you good reading.

—Michael E. Gerber
Co-Founder/Chairman
Michael E. Gerber Companies, Inc.
Carlsbad, California
www.michaelegerber.com/co-author

A NOTE FROM DR. FRANK

What if something you thought to be true turned out not to be? How soon would you want to know? If you are like most people you will say, "Right away! Bring it!" Keep that attitude because you are about to get the best adjustment of your life. What you know or were told was true about success in practice is not the whole story, and I am willing to bet that it is only half the story.

Until I read Michael E. Gerber's book, *The E-Myth: Why Most Small Businesses Don't Work and What to Do About It*, the truth for me was simple: Work hard, take great care of your patients, and your business and your money will take care of themselves. Nice illusion, brutal reality. The truth is business never just takes care of itself, and as for money, well, more about that later on in the book. Being a good doctor is not enough. To be successful, your business skills must be as competent as your clinical skills.

My name is Dr. Frank Sovinsky and as the co-author of the book you are reading, I invite you to engage in a conversation with us, a talk about you, and a fresh look at your practice. As a chiropractor, I know the pressure you face as a doctor. I know how it feels when patients reject your care plan or drop out of care before they get the results they want. I have felt the anxiety that a lack of new patients brings. I know what it is like to have staff mentally quit—but never physically leave—or to be held hostage in your own office because you don't know how to do the things they do. I understand your frustration with insurance companies, your stress over taxes, student loans, potential litigation, and mortgage payments. I understand that a challenging and unforgiving economy leaves you no room for error.

That's what this book is about. It's about hope, growth, and a real plan. A unique and personal strategy to set you free! Whether you are a student, new graduate, or seasoned chiropractor, the ideas and processes we are going to discuss in this book will change how you look at the business of chiropractic and help you get the results and personal practice fulfillment you have been seeking.

I would like to tell you that in my lifelong quest for truth and knowledge I discovered the solution for my practice frustration all on my own. But then again this is a book about truth, so here's the real story. One night as I droned on and on about my practice, my staff, and those patients who just don't appreciate all I do, my wife of six months, Cathy, walked over to me. I thought she was about to refill my wineglass, but she was about to empty it. When I looked up, I saw that she held what I later understood to be objects of revelation. In her right hand was a necklace that she had fashioned from a ribbon with a pacifier hanging from it, and in the other hand was that little blue book, *The E-Myth*.

"I am concerned that you might wear out your thumbs sucking on them, so here is a binky," she said, "and if you are ready to do something about our business, this book will show you how."

I read, we talked, she read, and I listened. Michael E. Gerber, in a very tangible way, changed our business strategy and transformed our lives. As he suggested, we went to work on our business, not in it. We lived and breathed the E-Myth way, and our practice transformed into a remarkably successful business driven by passion and supported by interlocking and interdependent systems. And because the E-Myth principles are universal, we have successfully transformed our chiropractic coaching company, DC Mentors, into a truly meaningful business that is impacting the lives of chiropractors and their patients worldwide.

Have you ever read something and felt as if the author were inside your head because the message seemed like it was meant just for you? Well, that's what it was like for me. And I must tell you that I learned something else as I read the E-Myth point of view: The truth does set you free, but it can make you miserable at first! One statement literally made my jaw drop. Michael said that I had essentially built a job for myself. I hated jobs. I didn't mind working—I've always worked hard—but I hated not being in charge, not really feeling in control of my own destiny. In school I thought that being a chiropractor and owning my own practice would finally give me that control. Michael was correct that I not only had a job, I was working for a lunatic who had no idea how to be an effective business owner.

Just like you, I became a chiropractor because I wanted to eliminate needless suffering in the world. I wanted to empower my patients and set them free physically, emotionally, and attitudinally through the philosophy, art, and science of chiropractic. But I never imagined or truly understood that I would need courses in business planning, growth, and management to be a successful doctor.

As a mentor I have heard every excuse for practice mediocrity. Doctors tell me that they want to be busy and successful, but not too busy. Ironic, isn't it? Success, like health, is a natural consequence of making the right choices and taking the right actions. Can you really be too healthy? Of course not, so how on earth can you be too successful? In the opening paragraph I asked you, "What if something you thought to be true turned out not to be? How soon would you want to know?" I thought I heard you say, "Right away! Bring it!" So here it is: If you don't become a better businessperson, you can never have the life you dreamed about when you were in school. I am not talking about abandoning your vision. I am talking about how to find the interference that is blocking that vision and showing you how to remove it. For things to get better, you have to get better.

Now, I join with Michael as the E-Myth Chiropractor. The choices and actions you take from this point forward will determine your success or define your struggle. If you are ready to do something about your business, this book will show you how. If you fully engage and commit to these ideas, you can look forward to enough time and resources to live and achieve your dream.

—Frank Sovinsky, DC
Co-Founder and CEO
DC Mentors
Tahoe City, California

PREFACE

Michael E. Gerber

I am not a chiropractor, though I have helped dozens of chiropractors reinvent their chiropractic practices over the past thirty-five years.

I like to think of myself as a thinker, maybe even a dreamer. Yes, I like to *do* things. But before I jump in and get my hands dirty, I prefer to think through what I'm going to do and figure out the best way to do it. I imagine the impossible, dream big, and then try to figure out how the impossible can become the possible. After that, it's about how to turn the possible into reality.

Over the years, I've made it my business to study how things work and how people work—specifically, how things and people work best together to produce optimum results. That means creating an organization that can do great things and achieve more than any other organization can.

This book is about how to produce the best results as a real-world chiropractor in the development, expansion, and *liberation* of your practice. In the process, you will come to understand what the practice of chiropractic—as a *business*—is, and what it isn't. If you keep focusing on what it isn't, you're destined for failure. But if you turn your sights on what it *is*, the tide will turn.

This book, intentionally small, is about big ideas. The topics we'll be discussing in this book are the very issues that chiropractors face daily in their practice. You know what they are: money, management, patients, and many more. My aim is to help you begin the exciting process of totally transforming the way you do business. As such, I'm confident that *The E-Myth Chiropractor* could well be the most important book on the practice of chiropractic as a business that you'll ever read.

Unlike other books on the market, my goal is not to tell you how to do the work you do. Instead, I want to share with you the E-Myth philosophy as a way to revolutionize the way you think about the work you do. I'm convinced that this new way of thinking is something chiropractors everywhere must adopt in order for their chiropractic practice to flourish during these trying times. I call it strategic thinking, as opposed to tactical thinking.

In strategic thinking, also called systems thinking, you, the chiropractor, will begin to think about your entire practice—the broad scope of it—instead of focusing on its individual parts. You will begin to see the end game (perhaps for the first time) rather than just the day-to-day routine that's consuming you—the endless, draining work I call "doing it, doing it, doing it."

Understanding strategic thinking will enable you to create a practice that becomes a successful business, with the potential to flourish as an even more successful enterprise. But in order for you to accomplish this, your practice, your business, and certainly your enterprise must work *apart* from you instead of *because* of you.

The E-Myth philosophy says that a highly successful chiropractic practice can grow into a highly successful chiropractic business, which in turn can become the foundation for an inordinately successful chiropractic enterprise that runs smoothly and efficiently *without* the chiropractor having to be in the office for ten hours a day, six days a week.

So what is "The E-Myth," exactly? The E-Myth is short for the Entrepreneurial Myth, which says that most businesses fail to fulfill their potential because most people starting their own business are not entrepreneurs at all. They're actually what I call *technicians suffering from an entrepreneurial seizure*. When technicians suffering from an entrepreneurial seizure start a chiropractic practice of their own, they almost always end up working themselves into a frenzy; their days are booked solid with appointments, one patient after another. These chiropractors are burning the candle at both ends, fueled by too much coffee and too little sleep, and most of the time, they can't even stop to think.

In short, the E-Myth says that most chiropractors don't own a true business—most own a job. They're doing it, doing it, doing it, hoping like hell to get some time off, but never figuring out how to get their business to run without them. And if your business doesn't run well without you, what happens when you can't be in two places at once? Ultimately, your practice will fail.

There are a number of prestigious schools throughout the world dedicated to teaching the science of chiropractic. The problem is they fail to teach the *business* of it. And because no one is being taught how to run a practice as a business, some chiropractors find themselves having to close their doors every year. You could be a world-class expert in sports injury and prevention, nutrition, pediatrics, or neurology, but when it comes to building a successful business all that specified knowledge matters exactly zilch.

The good news is that you don't have to be among the statistics of failure in the chiropractic profession. The E-Myth philosophy I am about to share with you in this book has been successfully applied to thousands of chiropractic practices just like yours with extraordinary results.

The key to transforming your practice—and your life—is to grasp the profound difference between going to work *on* your practice (systems thinker) and going to work *in* your practice (tactical thinker). In other words, it's the difference between going to work on your practice as an entrepreneur and going to work in your practice as a chiropractor.

The two are not mutually exclusive. In fact, they are essential to each other. The problem with most chiropractic practices is that the systems thinker—the entrepreneur—is completely absent. And so is the vision.

The E-Myth philosophy says that the key to transforming your practice into a successful enterprise is knowing how to transform yourself from successful chiropractic technician into successful technician-manager-entrepreneur. In the process, everything you do in your chiropractic practice will be transformed. The door is then open to turning it into the kind of practice it should be—a practice, a business, an enterprise of pure joy.

The E-Myth not only *can* work for you, it *will* work for you. In the process, it will give you an entirely new experience of your business and beyond.

To your future and your life. Good reading.

—Michael E. Gerber
Co-Founder/Chairman
Michael E. Gerber Companies, Inc.
Carlsbad, California
www.michaelegerber.com/co-author

ACKNOWLEDGMENTS

Michael E. Gerber

As always, and never to be forgotten, there are those who give of themselves to make my work possible.

To my dearest and most forgiving partner, wife, friend, and co-founder, Luz Delia Gerber, whose love and commitment takes me to places I would often not go unaccompanied.

To Jim Taylor, whose persistency and at times demonic, steady state of heart, made the impossible less improbable, and the possible, if not easy, more predictable than we hoped.

To Helen Chang, noble warrior, editor, brave soul, and sojourner, who covers all the bases we would have missed had she not been there. To Erich Broesel, our stand-alone graphic designer and otherwise visual genius who supported the creation of all things visual that will forever be all things Gerber, we thank you, deeply, for your continuous contribution of things both temporal and eternal. To Trish Beaulieu, wow, you are splendid. And to Nancy Ratkiewich, whose work has been essential for you who are reading this.

To Johanna Nilsson, who told us that social media was much, much more than just social, and then, with the grace G-d gave her, proved it every step of the way.

To those many, many dreamers, thinkers, storytellers, and leaders, whose travels with me in The Dreaming Room have given me life, breath, and pleasure unanticipated before we met. To those many participants in my life (you know who you are), thank you for taking me seriously, and joining me in this exhilarating quest.

And, of course, to my co-authors, all of you, your genius, wisdom, intelligence, and wit have supplied me with a grand view of the world, which would never have been the same without you.

Love to all.

ACKNOWLEDGMENTS

Dr. Frank Sovinsky

I am a rich man because of the extraordinary people in my life. To Cathy, my wife, partner, and the most remarkable, talented, loving person I have ever met, without whom none of my dreams would have manifested.

My deep gratitude to our best friends and partners, Dr. Douglas Sea and Dr. Cecile Thackeray, for their relentless commitment and contagious passion for helping us transform a generation of chiropractors. To Ellen Culver, DC Mentors' director of client services, for her loyalty, tireless effort, and commitment to our clients.

To my amazing daughter, Chenoa Farrell, for bringing out the dad gene and inspiring me with her philosophy and soul-stirring music. To my granddaughter, Farrell, for her smile, her love, and for showing me that legacy is not just a word.

To Patty Diana Kaul, my friend and mother-in-law, for sharing her daughter and being a fun part of our life.

I am indebted to all the chiropractors and staff whom I have had the privilege to work with, for having trusted the integrity of our process and adding to our purpose.

A special thanks to the members of DC Mentors Elite "Tribe." As they change the world one patient, one community at a time, they move me to dream on an unimaginable scale. Thank you all from the center of my being.

INTRODUCTION

Michael E. Gerber

A s I write this book, the recession continues to take its toll on American businesses. Like any other industry, chiropractic is not immune. Chiropractors all over the country are watching as patients defer visits for adjustments and wellness care. At a time when per capita disposable income is at an all-time low, many people are choosing not to spend their hard-earned money on chiropractic services for themselves and even for their children. As a result, chiropractic care moves from the realm of necessity to luxury, and regrettably, healthy lifestyles and preventive care become an expendable concern while industry revenue takes a sizable dip into the red.

Faced with a struggling economy and fewer and fewer patients, many chiropractors I've met are asking themselves, "Why did I ever become a chiropractor in the first place?"

And it isn't just a money problem. After 35 years of working with small businesses, many of them chiropractic practices, I'm convinced that the dissatisfaction experienced by countless chiropractors is not just about money. To be frank, the recession doesn't deserve all the blame, either. While the financial crisis our country is facing certainly hasn't made things any better, the problem started long before the economy tanked. Let's dig a little deeper. Let's go back to school.

Can you remember that far back? Whichever university or college of chiropractic you attended, you probably had some great teachers who helped you become the fine Doctor of Chiropractic you are. These schools excel at teaching the science of chiropractic; they'll teach you everything you need to know about the nervous system, musculoskeletal system, and systemic diseases. But what they *don't* teach is the consummate skill set needed to be a successful chiropractor, and they certainly don't teach what it takes to build a successful chiropractic enterprise.

Obviously, something is seriously wrong. The education that chiropractic professionals receive in school doesn't go far enough, deep enough, broad enough. Colleges of chiropractic don't teach you how to relate to the *enterprise* of chiropractic or to the *business* of chiropractic; they only teach you how to relate to the *practice* of chiropractic. In other words, they merely teach you how to be an *effective* rather than a *successful* chiropractor. Last time I checked, they weren't offering degrees in success. That's why most chiropractors are effective, but few are successful.

Although a successful chiropractor must be effective, an effective chiropractor does not have to be—and in most cases isn't—successful.

An effective chiropractor is capable of executing his or her duties with as much certainty and professionalism as possible.

A successful chiropractor, on the other hand, works balanced hours, has little stress, leads rich and rewarding relationships with friends and family, and has an economic life that is diverse, fulfilling, and shows a continuous return on investment.

A successful chiropractor finds time and ways to give back to the community but at little cost to his or her sense of ease.

A successful chiropractor is a leader, not simply someone who teaches patients how to care for themselves and protect their health, but a sage; a rich person (in the broadest sense of the word); a strong father, mother, wife, or husband; a friend, teacher, mentor, and spiritually grounded human being; and a person who can see clearly into all aspects of what it means to lead a fulfilling life.

So let's go back to the original question. Why did you become a chiropractor? Were you striving to just be an effective one, or did you dream about real and resounding success?

I don't know how you've answered that question in the past, but I am confident that once you understand the strategic thinking laid out in this book, you will answer it differently in the future.

If the ideas here are going to be of value to you, it's critical that you begin to look at yourself in a different, more productive way. I am suggesting that you go beyond the mere technical aspects of your daily job as a Doctor of Chiropractic and begin instead to think strategically about your chiropractic practice as both a business and an enterprise.

I often say that most *practices* don't work—the people who own them do. In other words, most chiropractic practices are jobs for the chiropractors who own them. Does this sound familiar? The chiropractor, overcome by an entrepreneurial seizure, has started his or her own practice, become his or her own boss, and now works for a lunatic!

The result: the chiropractor is running out of time, patience, and ultimately money. Not to mention paying the worst price anyone can pay for the inability to understand what a true practice is, what a true business is, and what a true enterprise is—the price of his or her life.

In this book I'm going to make the case for why you should think differently about what you do and why you do it. It isn't just the future of your chiropractic practice that hangs in the balance. It's the future of your life.

The E-Myth Chiropractor is an exciting departure from my other sole-authored books. In this book, an expert—a licensed chiropractor who has successfully applied the E-Myth to the development of his chiropractic practice—is sharing his secrets about how he achieved extraordinary results using the E-Myth paradigm. In addition to the time-tested E-Myth strategies and systems I'll be sharing with you, you'll benefit from the wisdom, guidance, and practical tips provided by a legion of chiropractors who've been in your shoes.

The problems that afflict chiropractic practices today don't only exist in the field of health care; the same problems are confronting every organization of every size, in every industry in every country in the world. *The E-Myth Chiropractor* is next in a new series of E-Myth Expert books that will serve as a launching pad for Michael E. Gerber Partners™ to bring a legacy of expertise to small, struggling businesses in *all* industries. This series will offer an exciting opportunity to understand and apply the significance of E-Myth methodology in both theory and practice to businesses in need of development and growth.

The E-Myth says that only by conducting your business in a truly innovative and independent way will you ever realize the unmatched joy that comes from creating a truly independent business, a business that works *without* you rather than *because* of you.

The E-Myth says that it is only by learning the difference between the work of a *business* and the business of *work* that chiropractors will be freed from the predictable and often overwhelming tyranny of the unprofitable, unproductive routine that consumes them on a daily basis.

The E-Myth says that what will make the ultimate difference between the success or failure of your chiropractic practice is first and foremost how you *think* about your business, as opposed to how hard you work in it.

So, let's think it through together. Let's think about those things—work, patients, money, time—that dominate the world of chiropractors everywhere.

Let's talk about planning. About growth. About management. About getting a life!

Let's think about improving your and your family's life through the development of an extraordinary practice. About getting the life you've always dreamed of but never thought you could actually have.

Envision the future you want, and the future is yours.

The Story of Steve and Peggy

Michael E. Gerber

You leave home to seek your fortune and, when you get it, you go home and share it with your family.

—Anita Baker

Every business is a family business. To ignore this truth is to court disaster.

This is true whether or not family members actually work in the business. Whatever their relationship with the business, every member of a chiropractor's family will be greatly affected by the decisions a chiropractor makes about the business. There's just no way around it.

Unfortunately, like most doctors, chiropractors tend to compartmentalize their lives. They view their practice as a profession—what they do—and therefore it's none of their family's business.

"This has nothing to do with you," says the chiropractor to his wife, with blind conviction. "I leave work at the office and family at home."

1

And with equal conviction, I say, "Not true!"

In actuality, your family and chiropractic practice are inextricably linked to one another. What's happening in your practice is also happening at home. Consider the following and ask yourself if each is true:

- If you're angry at work, you're also angry at home.
- If you're out of control in your chiropractic practice, you're equally out of control at home.
- If you're having trouble with money in your practice, you're also having trouble with money at home.
- If you have communication problems in your practice, you're also having communication problems at home.
- If you don't trust in your practice, you don't trust at home.
- If you're secretive in your practice, you're equally secretive at home.

And you're paying a huge price for it!

The truth is that your practice and your family are one—and you're the link. Or you should be. Because if you try to keep your practice and your family apart, if your practice and your family are strangers, you will effectively create two separate worlds that can never wholeheartedly serve each other. Two worlds that split each other apart.

Let me tell you the story of Steve and Peggy Walsh.

The Walshes met in college. They were lab partners in organic chemistry, Steve a pre-chiropractic student and Peggy pre-nursing. When their lab discussions started to wander beyond spectroscopy and carboxylic acids and into their personal lives, they discovered they had a lot in common. By the end of the course, they weren't just talking in class; they were talking on the phone every night . . . and *not* about organic chemistry.

Steve thought Peggy was absolutely brilliant, and Peggy considered Steve the most passionate man she knew. It wasn't long before they were engaged and planning their future together. A week after graduation, they were married in a lovely garden ceremony in Peggy's childhood home.

While Steve studied at a prestigious college of chiropractic, Peggy entered a nursing program nearby. Over the next few years, the couple worked hard to keep their finances afloat. They worked long hours and studied constantly; they were often exhausted and struggled to make ends meet. But through it all, they were committed to what they were doing and to each other.

After passing his state boards, Steve became an associate doctor in a busy practice while Peggy began working in a large hospital nearby. Soon afterward, the couple had their first son, and Peggy decided to take some time off from the hospital to be with him. Those were good years. Steve and Peggy loved each other very much, were active members in their church, participated in community organizations, and spent quality time together. The Walshes considered themselves one of the most fortunate families they knew.

But work became troublesome. Steve grew increasingly frustrated with the way the practice was run. "I want to go into business for myself," he announced one night at the dinner table. "I want to start my own practice."

Steve and Peggy spent many nights talking about the move. Was it something they could afford? Did Steve really have the skills necessary to make a chiropractic practice a success? Were there enough patients to go around? What impact would such a move have on Peggy's career at the local hospital, their lifestyle, their son, their relationship? They asked all the questions they thought they needed to answer before Steve went into business for himself ... but they never really drew up a concrete plan.

Finally, tired of talking and confident that he could handle whatever he might face, Steve committed to starting his own chiropractic practice. Because she loved and supported him, Peggy agreed, offering her own commitment to help in any way she could. So Steve quit his job, took out a second mortgage on their home, and leased a small office nearby.

In the beginning, things went well. A building boom had hit the town, and new families were pouring into the area. Steve had no trouble getting new patients. His practice expanded, quickly outgrowing his office.

Within a year, Steve had employed an office manager, Clarissa, to run the front desk and handle the administrative side of the business. He also hired a bookkeeper, Tim, to handle the finances. Steve was ecstatic with the progress his young practice had made. He celebrated by taking his wife and son on vacation to Italy.

Of course, managing a business was more complicated and time-consuming than working for someone else. Steve not only supervised all the jobs Clarissa and Tim did, but also was continually looking for work to keep everyone busy. When he wasn't scanning journals of chiropractic to stay abreast of what was going on in the field or fulfilling continuing-education requirements to stay current on the standards of care, he was going to the bank, wading through patient paperwork, or speaking with insurance companies (which usually degenerated into *arguing* with insurance companies). He also found himself spending more and more time on the telephone dealing with patient complaints and nurturing relationships.

As the months went by and more and more patients came through the door, Steve had to spend even more time just trying to keep his head above water.

By the end of its second year, the practice, now employing two full-time and two part-time people, had moved to a larger office downtown. The demands on Steve's time had grown with the practice.

He began leaving home earlier in the morning and returning later at night. He drank more. He rarely saw his son anymore. For the most part, Steve was resigned to the problem. He saw the hard work as essential to building the "sweat equity" he had long heard about.

Money was also becoming a problem for Steve. Although the practice was growing like crazy, money always seemed scarce when it was really needed. He had discovered that insurance companies were often slow to pay, and when they did, they cut his fee.

When Steve had worked for somebody else, he had been paid twice a month. In his own practice, he often had to wait—sometimes for months. He was still owed money on billings he had completed more than ninety days before.

When he complained to late-paying insurers, it fell on deaf ears. They would shrug, smile, and promise to do their best to review the claims, adding, "But your care plan does not meet medical necessity according to our guidelines." Of course, no matter how slowly Steve got paid, he still had to pay *his* people. This became a relentless problem. Steve often felt like a juggler dancing on a tightrope. A fire burned in his stomach day and night.

To make matters worse, Steve began to feel that Peggy was insensitive to his troubles. Not that he often talked to his wife about the practice. "Business is business" was Steve's mantra. "It's my responsibility to handle things at the office and Peggy's responsibility to take care of her own job and the family."

Peggy was working late hours at the hospital, and they'd brought in a nanny to help with their son. Steve couldn't help but notice that his wife seemed resentful, and her apparent lack of understanding baffled him. Didn't she see that he had a practice to take care of? That he was doing it all for his family? Apparently not.

As time went on, Steve became even more consumed and frustrated by his practice. When he went off on his own, he remembered saying, "I don't like people telling me what to do." But people were still telling him what to do. On one particularly frustrating morning, his office had to get an insurance authorization for a $57 cervical X-ray. It required a long-distance call and twenty-five minutes on hold. Steve was furious.

Not surprisingly, Peggy grew more frustrated by her husband's lack of communication. She cut back on her own hours at the hospital to focus on their family, but her husband still never seemed to be around. Their relationship grew tense and strained. The rare moments they *were* together were more often than not peppered by long silences—a far cry from the heartfelt conversations that had characterized their relationship's early days, when they'd talk into the wee hours of the morning.

Meanwhile, Tim, the bookkeeper, was also becoming a problem for Steve. Tim never seemed to have the financial information Steve needed to make decisions about payroll, patient billing, and general operating expenses, let alone how much money was available for Steve and Peggy's living expenses.

When questioned, Tim would shift his gaze to his feet and say, "Listen, Steve, I've got a lot more to do around here than you can imagine. It'll take a little more time. Just don't press me, okay?"

Overwhelmed by his own work, Steve usually backed off. The last thing Steve wanted was to upset Tim and have to do the books himself. He could also empathize with what Tim was going through, given the practice's growth over the past year.

Late at night in his office, Steve would sometimes recall his first years out of school. He missed the simple life he and his family had shared. Then, as quickly as the thoughts came, they would vanish. He had work to do and no time for daydreaming. "Having my own practice is a great thing," he would remind himself. "I simply have to apply myself, as I did in school, and get on with the job. I have to work as hard as I always have when something needed to get done."

Steve began to live most of his life inside his head. He began to distrust his people. They never seemed to work hard enough or to care about his practice as much as he did. If he wanted to go get something done, he usually had to do it himself.

Then one day, the office manager, Clarissa, quit in a huff, frustrated by the amount of work that her boss was demanding of her. Steve was left with a desk full of papers and a telephone that wouldn't stop ringing.

Clueless about the work Clarissa had done, Steve was overwhelmed by having to pick up the pieces of a job he didn't understand. His world turned upside down. He felt like a stranger in his own practice.

Why had he been such a fool? Why hadn't he taken the time to learn what Clarissa did in the office? Why had he waited until now?

Ever the trouper, Steve plowed into Clarissa's job with everything he could muster. What he found shocked him. Clarissa's work space was a disaster area! Her desk drawers were a jumble of papers, coins, pens, pencils, rubber bands, envelopes, business cards, fee slips, eye drops, and candy.

"What was she thinking?" Steve raged.

When he got home that night, even later than usual, he got into a shouting match with Peggy. He settled it by storming out of the house to get a drink. Didn't anybody understand him? Didn't anybody care what he was going through?

He returned home only when he was sure Peggy was asleep. He slept on the couch and left early in the morning, before anyone was awake. He was in no mood for questions or arguments.

When Steve got to his office the next morning, he immediately headed for the therapy room—maybe the cold laser could get rid of his throbbing headache.

What lessons can we draw from Steve and Peggy's story? I've said it once and I'll say it again: *Every business is a family business.* Your business profoundly touches all members of your family, even if they never set foot inside your office. Every business either gives to the family or takes from the family, just as individual family members do.

If the business takes more than it gives, the family is always the first to pay the price.

In order for Steve to free himself from the prison he created, he would first have to admit his vulnerability. He would have to confess to himself and his family that he really didn't know enough about his own practice and how to grow it.

Steve tried to do it all himself. Had he succeeded, had the practice supported his family in the style he imagined, he would have burst with pride. Instead, Steve unwittingly isolated himself, thereby achieving the exact opposite of what he sought.

He destroyed his life—and his family's life along with it.

Repeat after me: *Every business is a family business.*

Are you like Steve? I believe that all chiropractors share a common soul with him. You must learn that a business is only a business. It is not your life. But it is also true that your business can have a profoundly negative impact on your life unless you learn how to do it differently than most chiropractors do it—and definitely differently than Steve did it.

Steve's chiropractic practice could have served his and his family's life. But for that to happen, he would have had to learn how to master his practice in a way that was completely foreign to him.

Instead, Steve's practice consumed him. Because he lacked a true understanding of the essential strategic thinking that would have allowed him to create something unique, Steve and his family were doomed from day one.

This book contains the secrets that Steve should have known. If you follow in Steve's footsteps, prepare to have your life and business fall apart. But if you apply the principles we'll discuss here, you can avoid a similar fate.

Let's start with the subject of *money*. But, before we do, let's listen to the chiropractor's view about the story I just told you. Let's talk about how it's your story to write by Dr. Frank. ✤

It's Your Story to Write

Dr. Frank Sovinsky

Whether we like it or not, our lives will leave a mark on the universe. Each person's birth makes ripples that expand in our social environments: parents, siblings, relatives, and friends are affected by us, and as we grow up our actions leave a myriad of consequences, some intended, most not.

—Mihaly Csikszentmihalyi

Take a moment to step back from the routines of your practice and the rituals of your life. Take a deep breath. I urge you to quiet the chattering monkeys in your head because they are determined to distract you from the real work we are doing together. If you are thinking about your day or stuck on something from last week, you might miss the point of this chapter, and your story is too important to miss. So take another breath or two. It is in this moment that the right questions are born and the "right for you" answers wait. Are you ready? Good, let's begin.

9

When I look at your life as a chiropractor, I am filled with a sense of awe. I mean, you change the lives of so many people! When you entered this profession, you had a plethora of things you wanted to fix in the world, things you wanted to do, to have, and to become. Yet Michael and I want to know: to what scale do you want to impact the world?

Your pursuit of happiness has led you to this path of service called chiropractic practice. And it is on this path of service that you will fulfill your destiny. Yet this path has exposed, or will expose, an important truth. If you are going to make a difference and contribute to change in the world, then you must see your practice as an entrepreneur sees his or hers. You need to think like an entrepreneur thinks, ask the deeper questions that an entrepreneur asks, and you need to behave like an entrepreneur behaves.

You are reading this book because you know that choices shape your chances for success. The more you learn, the more perspectives you hear, the closer you come to closing the gap between where your practice is now and where you want it to be. You might be right on the edge of explosive growth and all it will take is one more push. You might be in a bit of a rut and have lost that loving feeling. Or you might be somewhere in between. You are here for the right reason—yours.

In chiropractic college I was obsessed with opening my own practice. All I could think about was getting through the academic gauntlet and on with real life. I just wanted to open those doors and let the people come in. Other classmates chose associateships, hoping to get real-world clinical and business experience, but that wasn't for me. Many still take that approach, and we will talk about that later because it is so important.

In E-Myth terms, the technician personality in me just wanted to adjust spines, change lives, and forget the rest. I told myself that a caring doctor should not get bogged down by the details of managing, marketing, and money. I just wanted to do what I wanted to do and never considered that my practice had needs, too.

When Michael wrote about management by abdication, not delegation, it got my attention. He said that I had hired people to do the work that I didn't know how to or care to do. How did he know? He wasn't a doctor. For a brief moment I actually thought that he had interviewed my wife, Cathy, and that she had told him about how I was running the family business straight into the ground. How else could he have known?

Why It Matters

You are, at this very moment, a vital part of a profession with an unprecedented vision. We are, by most standards, a young profession. The adjustment that was delivered by D.D. Palmer in 1895 has now been heard around the world thanks to our courageous and passionate predecessors. Today, many people in this profession work tirelessly to guarantee your right to practice and the right for patients to seek our help. But none of that matters if your practice doesn't work. Without your success, your story will never be told.

No one profession has all the answers, yet what you do matters to your patients. There are hundreds of thousands of people who suffer needlessly and will continue a life of drudgery and hopelessness unless you get busy doing what needs to be done, changing what needs to change, and taking action today, not tomorrow.

If you sense urgency in my voice, you are right. I have conducted surveys among chiropractic audiences and clients for the past decade. The question I pose is this: "Knowing what you know, would you suggest chiropractic as a career choice?"

I am saddened to tell you that 30 percent tell me, "No!" That really bothers me. It's not that I don't know why they respond this way or how to fix it. We will cover all of that in this book. It just saddens me that a passionate new doctor can become burned out after only five years or less in practice and that too many seasoned chiropractors have lost their zeal for this profession. It doesn't have to be this way.

If I just described you, this book is hope with a plan. If you are in the other 70 percent and would go back to school and do it all over again, then this book is preventive care.

Mirror, Mirror on the Wall

You have three relationships that shape your personal and professional life: the relationship you have with yourself, the relationships you have with others, and the relationship you have with your practice. Make no mistake about it, all of these relationships are interdependent, and the thing they all have in common is you.

You can assuage the pain of practice mediocrity through self-deception, and you can even ignore many of your relationship problems. Yet your practice is a measurable, palpable accounting of your inner journey, your leadership competence, and your work ethic.

Take another breath. We have more of your story to tell. Now think about the very moment when you were called to the stage to receive your diploma. Remember? How did you feel? Who was there with you? How did that moment make them feel? I know that on some level you understand that your actions and your emotions leave their marks on everyone around you. Michael just had us repeat with him, "Every business is a family business." Do you see how profound a perspective that is?

Your passion, your career aspirations, and your reaction to the wins and challenges you face in business have a ripple effect on those in your circle and beyond.

Now let's look at this same idea from a business perspective. Did you know that as a business owner you have stakeholders who have a vested financial, emotional, and, on some level, a spiritual connection to your success? It's easy to see that your spouse and children are inextricably tethered to your results, but what about your staff and their families and your patients?

Your staff is enrolled and emotionally involved because your practice fulfills them as human beings. The people who work alongside you want to grow and thrive, and they want economic certainty. They want to know if "their practice" will be around five years from today, even if you are not.

Your patients want to know if "their practice" will be there, ready to respond when they need it to, not just when you are in the mood. They want to know if "their practice" will be around five years from today.

What about the other stakeholders, like the banker who believed in your business plan and loaned you the money to start your practice? What about the vendors you buy from, the other businesses in your community, and, yes, even the coaches you hire?

You see, what you do has meaning to others. It affects them. This practice is not about you. Do you realize that? I bet you do. This is not a rhetorical exercise. I just want to be certain that you start this process of working on your business with the right attitude.

Practice Is a Full-Contact Game

The people you work for are those you leave behind each morning as you head out to your practice. Is the person who leaves the same person who comes home? While your intellect may try to compartmentalize your life, you do not live in emotional isolation. As Daniel Goleman pointed out in his pivotal research, your emotional intelligence is even more important than your IQ. And the first step to developing emotional acumen is to recognize that your moods and emotions affect others.

I'll bet you have had this experience or, as in my case, all of the following in the same day.

You get to the office and return a call to your accountant. She says, "The good news is that you made more money last quarter. The bad news is that we did not account for that growth, so you owe an extra $17,000. Can you get a check to me today?"

You walk out to the reception area. Your front desk person is late yet again, and you start to answer the phones while patients are arriving. Then you notice that the X-rays you need for yesterday's new patient's report of findings are nowhere to be seen. Your assistant finally shows up, and you get through the morning.

When you come back from lunch, you see that five people have canceled their appointments and two of them have asked for their records to be sent to another chiropractor.

The afternoon is busy. Things are looking up. Then your staff hands you a note letting you know that six people are waiting, and one of them has been there for more than thirty minutes and is not a happy camper. You have a headache. You even try to adjust yourself but can't quite get it to go, so, having made it through the day, you head for home.

Life happens, yet everything in this story is iatrogenic. You heard me, doctor-induced.

Now back to the myth of home and work separation. The message is clear. Wherever you go, there you are. Those who are close to you know you. They feel your pain and can see the frustration in your eyes. Burying emotions takes energy and puts up a wall between you and those you care about. Be open and honest with your feelings, but don't whine. Look for solutions, not sympathy.

I suggest that you download an "app" that prepares you for the office-home interface. Here are a couple of tips that I suggest to my clients. After office hours, clear your head and your emotional state so that you are prepared for the most important work you do: building strong, vibrant relationships with family and friends.

During the commute home listen to music or audiobooks, or just listen to the highway as your tires dance along the grooves. Sing songs like you do in the shower. What the heck, you are a rock star in your head, aren't you? Just be careful not to play your air guitar while driving!

As you reach for the door, pretend you are picking up your spouse for a date. Ask how his or her day went and listen! See your spouse! Let your kids crawl on you, and let them talk about their wild adventures. Then, if your lover asks you to share your wins, do so but never try to cover up your challenges. He or she knows you and can tell. Holding back leads to mistrust and misunderstanding, no matter how noble it may appear. Be real, and allow your partner to face the world with you.

I must issue a clear warning for the wise. Do not, I mean it, do not whine or drone on and on about your frustrations or you will get the "necklace of shame" that I described in "A Note from Dr. Frank."

Many of you have a spouse working with you in the practice. It is a blessing if you have a solid relationship and a practice killer if it is strained. You can't bicker at home and not have patients feel the tension in the office; no matter what you think, it is impossible. So fix it or work in separate businesses for the sake of the other stakeholders.

Adversity does not build character, it reveals it. A few years back I took a simple test designed by a 9-year-old. It got my attention. Here it is for your coaching pleasure: "The Logan Test."

Do you awake each morning excited about the day, not wanting to sleep any more than absolutely necessary?

Do you laugh as much as you once did?

Are you having as much fun in your personal life as you have in the past?

Tomorrow's health-care terrain will reward those of us who prepare ourselves and our practices for the new marketplace. In the movie "Groundhog Day," the character Phil Connors, played by Bill Murray, finally gets it. He awakens to the reality that he has power. He has the power of change.

The following chapters will give you that same power, the power to change. This is a perfect time to hear what Michael has to teach us about money. ✤

On the Subject
of Money

Michael E. Gerber

*There are three faithful friends: an old wife, an old dog, and
ready money.*

—Benjamin Franklin

H ad Steve and Peggy first considered the subject of *money* as
we will here, their lives could have been radically different.

Money is on the tip of every chiropractor's tongue, on
the edge (or at the very center) of every chiropractor's thoughts,
intruding on every part of a chiropractor's life.

With money consuming so much energy, why do so few
chiropractors handle it well? Why was Steve, like so many chiropractors, willing to entrust his financial affairs to a relative stranger?
Why is money scarce for most chiropractors? Why is there less
money than expected? And yet the demand for money is *always*
greater than anticipated.

What is it about money that is so elusive, so complicated, so
difficult to control? Why is it that every chiropractor I've ever met

hates to deal with the subject of money? Why are they almost always too late in facing money problems? And why are they constantly obsessed with the desire for more of it?

Money—you can't live with it and you can't live without it. But you'd better understand it and get your people to understand it. Because until you do, money problems will eat your practice for lunch.

You don't need an accountant or financial planner to do this. You simply need to prod your people to relate to money very personally. From the chiropractic technician at the front counter to the exam technician, they all should understand the financial impact of what they do every day in relationship to the profit and loss of the practice.

And so you must teach your people to think like owners, not like technicians or office managers or receptionists. You must teach them to operate like personal profit centers, with a sense of how their work fits in with the practice as a whole.

You must involve everyone in the practice with the topic of money—how it works, where it goes, how much is left, and how much everybody gets at the end of the day. You also must teach them about the four kinds of money created by the practice.

The Four Kinds of Money

In the context of owning, operating, developing, and exiting from a chiropractic practice, money can be split into four distinct but highly integrated categories:

- Income
- Profit
- Flow
- Equity

Failure to distinguish how the four kinds of money play out in your practice is a surefire recipe for disaster.

Important Note: Do not talk to your accountants or book-keepers about what follows; it will only confuse them and you. The information comes from the real-life experiences of thousands of small business owners, chiropractors included, most of whom were hopelessly confused about money when I met them. Once they understood and accepted the following principles, they developed a clarity about money that could only be called enlightened.

The First Kind of Money: Income

Income is the money chiropractors are paid by their practice for doing their job *in* the practice. It's what they get paid for going to work every day.

Clearly, if chiropractors didn't do their job, others would have to, and *they* would be paid the money the practice currently pays the chiropractors. Income, then, has nothing to do with *ownership*. Income is solely the province of *employee-ship*.

That's why to the chiropractor-as-*employee*, income is the most important form money can take. To the chiropractor-as-*owner*, however, it is the least important form money can take.

Most important; least important. Do you see the conflict? The conflict between the chiropractor-as-employee and the chiropractor-as-owner?

We'll deal with this conflict later. For now, just know that it is potentially the most paralyzing conflict in a chiropractor's life.

Failing to resolve this conflict will cripple you. Resolving it will set you free.

The Second Kind of Money: Profit

Profit is what's left over after a chiropractic practice has done its job effectively and efficiently. If there is no profit, the practice is doing something wrong.

However, just because the practice shows a profit does not mean it is necessarily doing all the right things in the right way. Instead, it just means that something was done right during or preceding the period in which the profit was earned.

The important issue here is whether the profit was intentional or accidental. If it happened by accident (which most profit does), don't take credit for it. You'll live to regret your impertinence.

If it happened intentionally, take all the credit you want. You've earned it. Because profit created intentionally, rather than by accident, is replicable—again and again. And your practice's ability to repeat its performance is the most critical ability it can have.

As you'll soon see, the value of money is a function of your practice's ability to produce it in predictable amounts at an above-average return on investment.

Profit can be understood only in the context of your practice's purpose, as opposed to *your* purpose as a chiropractor. Profit, then, fuels the forward motion of the practice that produces it. This is accomplished in four ways:

- Profit is *investment capital* that feeds and supports growth.
- Profit is *bonus capital* that rewards people for exceptional work.
- Profit is *operating capital* that shores up money shortfalls.
- Profit is *return-on-investment* capital that rewards you, the chiropractor-owner, for taking risks.

Without profit, a chiropractic practice cannot subsist, much less grow. Profit is the fuel of progress.

If a practice misuses or abuses profit, however, the penalty is much like having no profit at all. Imagine the plight of a chiropractor who has way too much return-on-investment capital and not enough investment capital, bonus capital, and operating capital. Can you see the imbalance this creates?

The Third Kind of Money: Flow

Flow is what money *does* in a chiropractic practice, as opposed to what money *is*. Whether the practice is large or small, money tends to move erratically through it, much like a pinball. One minute it's there; the next minute it's not.

Flow can be even more critical to a practice's survival than profit, because a practice can produce a profit and still be short of money. Has this ever happened to you? It's called profit on paper rather than in fact.

No matter how large your practice, if the money isn't there when it's needed, you're threatened—regardless of how much profit you've made. You can borrow it, of course. But money acquired in dire circumstances is almost always the most expensive kind of money you can get.

Knowing where the money is and where it will be when you need it is a critically important task of both the chiropractor-as-employee and the chiropractor-as-owner.

Rules of Flow

You will learn no more important lesson than the huge impact flow can have on the health and survival of your chiropractic practice, let alone your business or enterprise. The following two rules will help you understand why this subject is so critical.

1. **The First Rule of Flow states that your income statement is static, while the flow is dynamic.** Your income statement is a snapshot, while the flow is a moving picture. So, while your income statement is an excellent tool for analyzing your practice *after* the fact, it's a poor tool for managing it in the heat of the moment.

Your income statement tells you (1) how much money you're spending and where, and (2) how much money you're receiving and from where.

Flow gives you the same information as the income statement, plus it tells you *when* you're spending and receiving money. In other words, flow is an income statement moving through time. And that is the key to understanding flow. It is about management in real time. How much is coming in? How much is going out? You'd like to know this daily, or even by the hour if possible. Never by the week or month.

You must be able to forecast flow. You must have a flow plan that helps you gain a clear vision of the money that's out there next month and the month after that. You must also pinpoint what your needs will be in the future.

Ultimately, however, when it comes to flow, the action is always in the moment. It's about *now*. The minute you start to meander away from the present, you'll miss the boat.

Unfortunately, few chiropractors pay any attention to flow until it dries up completely and slow pay becomes no pay. They are oblivious to this kind of detail until, say, patients announce that they won't pay for this or that. That gets a chiropractor's attention because the expenses keep on coming.

When it comes to flow, most chiropractors are flying by the proverbial seat of their pants. No matter how many people you hire to take care of your money, until you change the way you think about it, you will always be out of luck. No one can do this for you.

Managing flow takes attention to detail. But when flow is managed, your life takes on an incredible sheen. You're swimming with the current, not against it. You're in charge!

2. **The Second Rule of Flow states that money seldom moves as you expect it to.** But you do have the power to change that, provided you understand the two primary sources of money as it comes in and goes out of your chiropractic practice.

The truth is, the more control you have over the *source* of money, the more control you have over its flow. The sources of money are both inside and outside your practice.

Money comes from *outside* your practice in the form of receivables, reimbursements, investments, and loans.

Money comes from *inside* your practice in the form of payables, taxes, capital investments, and payroll. These are the costs associated with attracting patients, delivering your services, operations, and so forth.

Few chiropractors see the money going *out* of their practice as a source of money, but it is.

When considering how to spend money in your practice, you can save—and therefore make—money in three ways:

- Do it more effectively.
- Do it more efficiently.
- Stop doing it altogether.

By identifying the money sources inside and outside your practice, and then applying these methods, you will be immeasurably better at controlling the flow in your practice.

But what are these sources? They include how you

- manage your services;
- buy supplies and equipment;
- compensate your people;
- plan people's use of time;
- determine the direct cost of your services;
- increase the number of patients seen;
- manage your work;
- collect reimbursements and receivables; and
- countless more.

In fact, every task performed in your practice (and ones you haven't yet learned how to perform) can be done more efficiently and effectively, dramatically reducing the cost of doing business. In the process, you will create more income, produce more profit, and balance the flow.

The Fourth Kind of Money: Equity

Sadly, few chiropractors fully appreciate the value of equity in their chiropractic practice. Yet equity is the second most valuable asset any chiropractor will ever possess. (The first most valuable asset is, of course, your life. More on that later.)

Equity is the financial value placed on your chiropractic practice by a prospective buyer.

Thus, your *practice* is your most important product, not your services. Because your practice has the power to set you free. That's right. Once you sell your practice—providing you get what you want for it—you're free!

Of course, to enhance your equity, to increase your practice's value, you have to build it right. You have to build a practice that works. A practice that can become a true business and a business that can become a true enterprise. A practice/business/enterprise that can produce income, profit, flow, and equity better than any other chiropractor's practice can.

To accomplish that, your practice must be designed so that it can do what it does systematically and predictably, every single time.

The Story of McDonald's

Let me tell you the most unlikely story anyone has ever told you about the successful building of a chiropractic practice, business, and enterprise. Let me tell you the story of Ray Kroc.

You might be thinking, "What on earth does a hamburger stand have to do with my practice? I'm not in the hamburger business; I'm a chiropractor."

Yes, you are. But by practicing chiropractic as you have been taught, you've abandoned any chance to expand your reach, help more patients, or improve your services the way they must be improved if the practice of chiropractic—and your life—is going to be transformed.

In Ray Kroc's story lies the answer.

Kroc called his first McDonald's restaurant "a little money machine." That's why thousands of franchisees bought it. And the reason it worked? Kroc demanded consistency, so that a hamburger in Philadelphia would be an advertisement for one in Peoria. In fact, no matter where you bought a McDonald's hamburger in the 1950s, the meat patty was guaranteed to weigh exactly 1.6 ounces, with a diameter of 3⅝ inches. It was in the McDonald's Operations Manual.

Did Kroc succeed? You know he did! And so can you, once you understand his methods. Consider just one part of his story.

In 1954, Kroc made his living selling the five-spindle Multimixer milkshake machine. He heard about a hamburger stand in San Bernardino, California, that had eight of his machines in operation, meaning it could make forty shakes simultaneously. This he had to see.

Kroc flew from Chicago to Los Angeles, then drove sixty miles to San Bernardino. As he sat in his car outside Mac and Dick McDonald's restaurant, he watched as lunch customers lined up for bags of hamburgers.

In a revealing moment, Kroc approached a strawberry blonde in a yellow convertible. As he later described it, "It was not her sex appeal but the obvious relish with which she devoured the hamburger that made my pulse begin to hammer with excitement."

Passion.

In fact, it was the french fry that truly captured his heart. Before the 1950s, it was almost impossible to buy fries of consistent quality. Kroc changed all that. "The french fry," he once wrote, "would become almost sacrosanct for me, its preparation a ritual to be followed religiously."

Passion and preparation.

The potatoes had to be just so—top-quality Idaho russets, eight ounces apiece, deep-fried to a golden brown, and salted with a shaker that, as Kroc put it, kept going "like a Salvation Army girl's tambourine."

As Kroc soon learned, potatoes too high in water content—and even top-quality Idaho russets varied greatly in water content—will come out soggy when fried. And so Kroc sent out teams of workers, armed with hydrometers, to make sure all his suppliers were producing potatoes in the optimal solids range of 20 to 23 percent.

Preparation and passion. Passion and preparation. Look those words up in the dictionary and you'll see Kroc's picture. Can you envision your picture there?

Do you understand what Kroc did? Do you see why he was able to sell thousands of franchises? Kroc knew the true value of equity, and unlike Steve from our story, Kroc went to work *on* his business rather than *in* his business. He knew the hamburger wasn't his product—McDonald's was!

So what does *your* chiropractic practice need to do to become a little money machine? What is the passion that will drive you to build a practice that works—a turnkey system like Ray Kroc's?

Equity and the Turnkey System

What's a turnkey system? And why is it so valuable to you? To better understand it, let's look at another example of a turnkey system that worked to perfection: the recordings of Frank Sinatra.

Frank Sinatra's records were to him as McDonald's restaurants were to Ray Kroc. They were part of a turnkey system that allowed Sinatra to sing to millions of people without having to be there himself.

Sinatra's recordings were a dependable turnkey system that worked predictably, systematically, automatically, and effortlessly to produce the same results every single time—no matter where they were played, and no matter who was listening.

Regardless of where Frank Sinatra was, his records just kept on producing income, profit, flow, and equity, over and over … and still do! Sinatra needed only to produce the prototype recording, and the system did the rest.

Kroc's McDonald's is another prototypical turnkey solution, addressing everything McDonald's needs to do in a basic, systematic way so that anyone properly trained by McDonald's can successfully reproduce the same results.

And this is where you'll realize your equity opportunity: in the way your practice does business, in the way your practice systematically does what you intend it to do, and in the development of your turnkey system—a system that works even in the hands of ordinary people (and chiropractors less experienced than you) to produce extraordinary results.

Remember:

- If you want to build vast equity in your practice, then go to work *on* your practice, building it into a business that works every single time.

- Go to work *on* your practice to build a totally integrated turnkey system that delivers exactly what you promised every single time.

- Go to work *on* your practice to package it and make it stand out from the chiropractic practices you see everywhere else.

Here is the most important idea you will ever hear about your practice and what it can potentially provide for you:

The value of your equity is directly proportional to how well your practice works. And how well your practice works is directly proportional to the effectiveness of the systems you have put into place upon which the operation of your practice depends.

Whether money takes the form of income, profit, flow, or equity, the amount of it—and how much of it stays with you—invariably boils down to this. Money, happiness, life—it all depends on how well your practice works. Not on your people, not on you, but on the system.

Your practice holds the secret to more money. Are you ready to learn how to find it?

Earlier in this chapter, I alerted you to the inevitable conflict between the chiropractor-as-employee and the chiropractor-as-owner.

It's a battle between the part of you working *in* the practice and the part of you working *on* the practice. Between the part of you working for income and the part of you working for equity.

Here's how to resolve this conflict:

- Be honest with yourself about whether you're filling *employee* shoes or *owner* shoes.

- As your practice's key employee, determine the most effective way to do the job you're doing, *and then document that job*.

- Once you've documented the job, create a strategy for replacing yourself with someone else (another chiropractor) who will then use your documented system exactly as you do.

- Have your new employees manage the newly delegated system. Improve the system by quantifying its effectiveness over time.

- Repeat this process throughout your practice wherever you catch yourself acting as employee rather than owner.

- Learn to distinguish between ownership work and employee-ship work every step of the way.

Master these methods, understand the difference between the four kinds of money, develop an interest in how money works in your practice . . . and then watch it flow in with the speed and efficiency of a perfectly delivered adjustment.

Now let's take another step in our strategic thinking process. Let's look at the subject of *planning*. But first, let's listen to what Dr. Frank has to say about money. ✤

CHAPTER

4

What You Do With Money Changes Everything

Dr. Frank Sovinsky

Money is a great power—because, in a free or even semi-free society, it is a frozen form of productive energy. And therefore, the spending of money is a grave responsibility.

—Ayn Rand

You have life insurance that protects your family if you die before you reach your peak earning years. But what if you live? Will they be able to enjoy an affluent lifestyle filled with opportunities and still have financial security?

I know you want to provide this kind of life assurance, and you can if you reconcile your feelings about money with the reality of money.

As a chiropractor, you are exposed to more than your share of half-truths, myths, and complete nonsense on the subject of money, how to get it, and how to keep it. We seem to be a magnet for attracting the magical mystery tour of happiness gurus and dispensers of hidden secrets revealed! And yes, sometimes we fall prey to unscrupulous moneychangers.

I do know this about you: You have integrity. And you are fast developing the mental horsepower and critical thinking necessary to guide your family's business.

Most of our feelings about money stem from two dangerous half-truths. The first one is expressed by the mantra: "If I do the right thing, money will just take care of itself." Money never takes care of itself.

The second half-truth is the belief that "If I had more money, it would change everything in my life." Money doesn't change everything. What you do with money changes everything.

This chapter is the next upgrade to developing your E-Myth mindset. Before you *do* the right thing with money, you have to think about money from the perspective of the chiropractor-as-owner, not the myopic vision of the chiropractor-as-employee. This is such a big distinction that I don't want you to miss it.

There's something else I know about you: You have a compassionate, nurturing heart for people. The best way I have found to describe you is the phrase "social-entrepreneur." Social because you are driven by an altruistic need to eliminate suffering and to teach healthy living; entrepreneur because you are a business owner.

As social-entrepreneurs we measure success in terms of the impact we have on the lives of our patients, on our community, and on society. Yet money is the fuel that your practice needs to sustain that vision and to succeed in this mission.

As health-care providers, our altruistic nature can conflict with the utilitarian reality of owning a business. Making a profit is not incompatible with your social obligation. In fact, it is essential.

Two Voices Becoming One

You have two voices in your head—well, some of us have a few more, but that's another book. These two voices and personalities have distinct psychological needs and disparate mental frames about success, happiness, and how best to run your practice.

Michael writes that the conflict between the chiropractor-as-employee and the chiropractor-as-owner needs to be understood, appreciated, and resolved. I couldn't agree more.

These two personalities look at money very differently. If you don't put the right one in charge of making the strategic decisions about money, nothing else will change in your life. You will be sentenced to a long career, plodding along, doing it, doing it, and doing it until you can't.

The chiropractor-as-employee sees a paycheck. He knows that if he sees more patients this week, his production, and hopefully his collection, will go up and his paycheck will be sizable. To him, success is that simple: more visits, more money.

The chiropractor-as-employee looks for bonuses and sees unexpected income and personal injury settlement money as a reward for a job well done. He might even rationalize that production, though not collected, is as good as money in his hands, so why not spend it? Yes, the employee feels entitled to spend it any way he feels. Toys and trips and treasures, oh my!

The chiropractor-as-owner sees the "collected money" and profit as leverage. To him, this is an investment opportunity for the business. He knows that more patient visits and higher production are only two data points, and that there are at least twenty-five other quantifiable measurements to be collected and analyzed so that he can forecast and make the necessary innovations and investments into the practice.

He plans to master his understanding of the business of chiropractic practice and build systems around the four kinds of money Michael just described.

The chiropractor-as-employee personality looks for safety and comfort in the numbers. He is emotionally dependent upon them. He only has a good day when he sees more patients or has a few more "new ones." Statistical fluctuations make him fearful, and when emotions are high, logic is low.

Always looking to get a bigger paycheck, he becomes obsessed with cost-cutting instead of expanding his market share and the quality of his service. So he doesn't hire the next staff member or replace the one who left. He only attends professional development seminars if they are required for his relicensing. The chiropractor-as-employee retreats to the safety of the old practice when economic challenges hit him.

The chiropractor-as-owner takes calculated risks for the sake of the business. He views statistical fluctuations as a byproduct of the practice's previous efforts, and uses it to forecast and make course corrections. Logic is high, emotion is low.

Campus Life Carries Over

If you are a student, I want you to see how this chiropractor-as-employee mentality might be playing out in your campus life. In the previous chapter, Michael said that money comes from outside a practice in the form of receivables, investments, and loans. You have money flowing into your life from either a student loan, a family member who loaned you money or cosigned a loan, a spouse who is working, or all of the above.

The truth about a loan is this: you get to pay it back! Starting right now, we want you to get the E-Myth philosophy about money and develop your critical thinking along with your education.

We need to talk about entitlement. When you get student loan money, it is not a paycheck to spend. It is working capital for your future enterprise. I realize you have to eat and sleep, buy books and pay your tuition. I know some of you are frugal, and I know some of you buy toys and trips with that money.

This is not your father speaking. This is the E-Myth Chiropractor. If you are in the habit of rationalizing your use of these precious dollars on toys, gear, or spring break, let me give you my famous five-second coaching hint. **Stop it!**

This habit carries over into life after graduation and will kill any chance of building a successful career. I watch chiropractors in their fifties behaving the same way they did as students. The cult of optimism, the one that says everything always works out for the better given enough time, has too many doctors sitting on the shoreline waiting for their ship to come in.

So learn to think like the chiropractor-as-owner thinks. Act like the chiropractor-as-owner would act. Get the best price available on books and computers. Choose seminars that will feed your clinical prowess and your business acumen. If you want to take a trip or buy a new mountain bike, get a part-time job. This is the principle.

Every dollar you receive from a loan is a "certificate of trust." Continue to be trustworthy and the world will respond in kind.

The "B" Word

The E-Myth path is paved by systems, systems, and then systems. The solution for your money attitude and behavior is to systematize the work of money in your practice and at home. I call a budget the "B" word because most people resist making one, and few ever follow one. Remember: Every business is a family business.

The first step is to get your household budget out in the light. Look at your fixed and variable costs over the last year. Do this with your spouse in real time, when the two of you can work on this together. Money disputes continue to fill divorce courts. It makes no sense to cross the finish line alone. Get the number and make it a weekly system. Follow the budget until it is time to review—usually every six months.

Do the same thing with your business. Look at your fixed and variable costs to keep your practice open and growing. Remember, the truth will set you free eventually, but it just might make you miserable at first.

Like a diet, this is not meant to limit you. It is intended to liberate you from the drama of consumerism. You will need to make sure that the chiropractor-as-employee is committed to the budget and the chiropractor-as-owner uses the budget.

We want you to create a way of consuming and a habit for producing. You see, a consumer is someone who spends more than he or she produces. It's called consumer debt for this reason. The BMW, the big starter house, or the cruise in the Bahamas that you put on a credit card is consumer debt. As part of your diet, I suggest you use credit cards only where required. It's amazing that some places actually discourage cash! In a pre-emancipation celebration, our clients take out all but one or two credit cards and cut them, crush them, or destroy them.

Credit cards distance you emotionally from the reality of the transaction. Studies in the field of neuro-economics confirm that we are motivated by loss aversion. These studies further suggest that the more removed we are from money transactions, the less responsible we are. We don't feel the pain, the loss of our hard-earned money.

The next time you are paying for lunch, purchasing something in a convenience store or mall, whip out that wallet or dig in the purse and take out real money. Then your emotional intelligence can play a role in the impulse buy. Be frugal, not parsimonious. To learn about money as a system, go to www.michaelegerber.com/co-author.

Money as a Tool

Money is a tool. In gifted hands, it can sculpt a masterpiece and make dreams become reality. In the hands of a novice, it makes junk art. Let's look at how money can be a tool in your practice.

Business loans are necessary debt. You must have working capital in order to get a return on the investment of your time and talent. Now that you have decided to work on your business, you may need a line of credit to give your practice a face-lift or to invest in technology and mentoring. And you will need to invest in programs that upgrade you and your team's soft skills. More about that later in the book.

Undercapitalization and unrealistic expectations keep most practices in the infancy stage. And if they do happen to survive and make it to adolescence, the financial whiplash takes the practice all the way back to infancy. Doctors who open on a shoestring struggle the rest of their careers as this shoestring becomes a noose tightening ever so slightly month after month.

Equity—the Golden Ticket

I admit I like the original film *Willy Wonka and the Chocolate Factory*. Imagine how easy it would be if all you had to do was be a good boy or girl, eat lots of chocolate, and find the Golden Ticket! Now back to reality.

In the last chapter, Michael described the end game and underscored the fourth kind of money: equity. Equity is your Golden Ticket! He said, "Equity is the financial value placed on your chiropractic practice by a prospective buyer." Equity, therefore, is the product that you create. It is the consequence of working on the right things. We want you to build it right, build it solid, and make it secure enough to thrive regardless of the economy.

When I talk to chiropractors about leaving their practices one day, I get two strong and predictable reactions. Those who are struggling nod their heads and say, "I can't wait to retire," then they look down and say, "but I can't afford to."

That look bothers me. If that is you, please lift your head. The good news is that you are reading this book. That tells me you've still got game. I am determined to coach you during this halftime break. Hold on, because the second half is about to start, and I want you to play a different game—one that's worth playing.

The other reaction I get when I suggest that a doctor leave his practice is surprise, followed by a quizzical look as if I am insane. Surprised doctors wonder why anyone would ever stop doing something they love to do. I understand that, and I get that what you do matters. I loved my patients and my staff; I still do. Yet I want you to see another perspective.

I am not trying to push you out, I am trying to open you up. I am trying to get you to the point in your business where you really have that choice. That's as honest as I can be. I built equity and I left. I am asked nearly every day if I miss practicing. My answer is simple: "No. If I thought I would miss it, I wouldn't have left." It was time for my next creative act.

Equity is real. You can touch it. You can play with it. You can re-create with it. My wife, Cathy, and I wanted to celebrate our equity moment. We traveled to Cairo, Egypt, and boarded a luxury vessel that took us to the ancient wonders along the Nile River. I'm a real history nerd. The yacht only accommodated thirty people, so it was intimate. The majority of our fellow passengers were medical doctors and their spouses in their late sixties, and I can guarantee that they had not read *The E-Myth Physician*.

The conversations always started with, "What do you do?" I love that question, and I love the meaningful dialogue that can follow. When I got around to sharing that I had just sold our business, they opened up. They asked how someone so young could afford to do that. I must say my retort was just a bit sassy: "Because I had something to sell."

One by one they told me that they wished they could sell their practices, but because of their contracts with HMOs and PPOs, their practice had no resale value! That didn't surprise me. They didn't have a systematized practice to sell. I could see in their eyes that they still had a job, they had some money, but they were doing it, doing it, doing it, not because they wanted to, but because they needed to.

I am telling you this story not to impress you but to touch a truth. I want you to have options. The timeline for your own version of our Nile River expedition is up to you. Do you have another creative act that needs to be birthed? That's my truth. What's yours?

There will be a time when you will leave your business. It's really that simple. Do you want to be in control of that day? I suspect that was a rhetorical question, so let me rephrase it. How about this: Let's put you in control of that day.

We build equity through our processes and systems. This equity is fluid and flows to the buyer of the business, and it guarantees that patient care is never compromised. How substantial will your equity be? It depends upon the choices and actions you take starting now.

Today we have adopted the buzz phrase "patient-centered care," and we will talk a little more on the subject later. What I want you to understand is that systems guarantee a patient-centered experience, and give your business real value and healthy equity.

The players, staff, and doctor do change, yet the game is still on in a big way. While it is true that you and your staff will develop remarkable and rewarding relationships with your patients and their families, you need to ensure that the essence of your care passes forward. This is what legacy is all about.

Patients want, need, and deserve to know they will get their adjustments on time, every time. They want predictability in a chaotic world. They want rational care plans and affordable services.

To ensure that your ethics and professionalism transfer, get your business clean and clear. Your clinical systems, including technique protocols, diagnostics, outcome assessments, and templates for care plans, need to be documented. Financial systems, including policies, insurance alliances, and payment options, need to be documented so that they are delivered today and can transfer without a hiccup down the road.

How Real Is Real Estate?

So that the day after tomorrow has a happy ending for you, I want to bring one more important perspective. The world has shifted on its financial axis. Security has been redefined. Let's get critical and put a fine point on a common misconception about owning your own building or office suite.

One of the biggest threats I see that undermines practice equity is the obsession doctors have with owning their office space. They see purchasing an office suite or free-standing building as a strategy to avoid wasting money paying rent, as an investment opportunity, and as a source of income by leasing space.

How real is the real estate these days? As we are writing this book, the housing crisis continues and it is anyone's guess when it will bottom out. Regardless of when or how complete this turnaround will be we can agree that your financial security should be in your control, not left to the real estate and banking marketplaces.

Too many doctors I talk to thought that their retirement nest egg was guaranteed because of the equity in their building. Sadly, they followed the logic of the 1970s and 1980s. They did not build practice equity. These same chiropractors have woken up to the reality that their building was at one time in a prime location, but now urban blight or economic downturn has eaten away at the value.

So keep your mind open for the next few paragraphs and then ruminate over the message. The advice that follows is counterintuitive and against the grain of mainstream advisors. Are you ready?

I predict that bankers who will make the decision to loan money to the buyer of your business will be hesitant to make loans big enough for the equity in your practice and the real estate purchase. One or the other will be devalued.

Having observed and studied the behavior of chiropractors for over thirty years, I want to add one more psychological perspective. Being a landlord or taking on the role of a property manager requires a whole other set of systems and focus. I suggest that you put all of your energy into building a practice worth talking about and transforming it into a business with a healthy bottom line and equity.

In chiropractic we talk about adapting to the environment as a key to a vibrant life. Well, now it's time for you to adapt and adopt better financial habits.

Together we will continue to build the neurological scaffolding necessary to remodel your thinking about the business of chiropractic practice. This is the perfect place to see what Michael has to say about planning. ✤

5

On the Subject
of Planning

Michael E. Gerber

Luck is good planning, carefully executed.

—Anonymous

A nother obvious oversight revealed in Steve and Peggy's story was the absence of true planning.

Every chiropractor starting his or her own practice must have a plan. You should never begin to see patients without a plan in place. But, like Steve, most chiropractors do exactly that.

A chiropractor lacking a vision is simply someone who goes to work every day. Someone who is just doing it, doing it, doing it. Busy, busy, busy. Maybe making money, maybe not. Maybe getting something out of life, maybe not. Taking chances without really taking control.

The plan tells anyone who needs to know *how we do things here*. The plan defines the objective and the process by which you will attain it. The plan encourages you to organize tasks into functions, and then helps people grasp the logic of each of those functions. This in turn permits you to bring new employees up to speed quickly.

There are numerous books and seminars on the subject of prac-tice management, but they focus on making you a better chiropractor. I want to teach you something else that you've never been taught before: how to be a manager. It has nothing to do with conven-tional practice management and everything to do with thinking like an entrepreneur.

The Planning Triangle

As we discussed in the Preface, every chiropractic practice is a company, every chiropractic business is a company, and every chiro-practic enterprise is a company. Yet the difference between the three is extraordinary. Although all three may offer chiropractic services, how they do what they do is completely different.

The trouble with most companies owned by chiropractors is that they are dependent on the chiropractor. That's because they're a practice—the smallest, most limited form a company can take. Practices are formed around the technician, whether chiropractor or roofer.

You may choose in the beginning to form a practice, but you should understand its limitations. The company called a *practice* depends on the owner—that is, the chiropractor. The company called a *business* depends on other people plus a system by which that business does what it does. Once your practice becomes a business, you can replicate it, turning it into an *enterprise*.

Consider the example of Sea Chiropractic. The patients don't come in asking for Dr. Douglas Sea, although he is one of the top chiropractors around. After all, he can only handle so many cases a day and be in only one location at a time.

Yet he wants to offer his high-quality services to more people in the community. If he has reliable systems in place—systems that any qualified associate chiropractor can learn to use—he has created a business and it can be replicated. Douglas can then go on to offer his services—which demand his guidance, not his presence—in a multitude of different settings. He can open dozens of chiropractic practices, none of which need Dr. Douglas Sea himself, except in the role of entrepreneur.

Is your chiropractic company going to be a practice, a business, or an enterprise? Planning is crucial to answering this all-important question. Whatever you choose to do must be communicated by your plan, which is really three interrelated plans in one. We call it the Planning Triangle, and it looks like this:

- The Business Plan
- The Practice Plan
- The Completion Plan

The three plans form a triangle, with the business plan at the base, the practice plan in the center, and the completion plan at the apex.

The
Completion
Plan

The Practice Plan

The Business Plan

The business plan determines *who* you are (the business), the practice plan determines *what* you do (the specific focus of your chiropractic practice), and the completion plan determines *how* you do it (the fulfillment process).

By looking at the planning triangle, we see that the three critical plans are interconnected. The connection between them is established by asking the following questions:

- Who are we?
- What do we do?
- How do we do it?

Who are we? is purely a strategic question.
What do we do? is both a strategic and a tactical question.
How do we do it? is both a strategic and a tactical question.

Strategic questions shape the vision and destiny of your business, of which your practice is only one essential component. Tactical questions turn that vision into reality. Thus, strategic questions provide the foundation for tactical questions, just as the base provides the foundation for the middle and apex of your planning triangle.

First ask: What do we do and how do we do it … *strategically?*

And then: What do we do and how do we do it … *practically?*

Let's look at how the three plans will help you develop your practice.

The Business Plan

Your business plan will determine what you choose to do in your chiropractic practice and the way you choose to do it. Without a business plan, your practice can do little more than survive. And even that will take more than a little luck.

Without a business plan, you're treading water in a deep pool with no shore in sight. You're working against the natural flow.

I'm not talking about the traditional business plan that is taught in business schools. No, this business plan reads like a story—the most important story you will ever tell.

Your business plan must clearly describe

- the business you are creating;
- the purpose it will serve;
- the vision it will pursue;
- the process through which you will turn that vision into a reality; and
- the way money will be used to realize your vision.

Build your business plan with *business* language, not *practice* language (the language of the chiropractor). Make sure the plan focuses on matters of interest to your lenders and shareholders rather than just your technicians. It should rely on demographics and psychographics to tell you who buys and why; it should also include projections for return on investment and return on equity. Use it to detail both the market and the strategy through which you intend to become a leader in that market, not as a chiropractor but as a business enterprise.

The business plan, though absolutely essential, is only one of three critical plans every chiropractor needs to create and implement. Now let's take a look at the practice plan.

The Practice Plan

The practice plan includes everything a chiropractor needs to know, have, and do in order to deliver his or her promise to a patient on time, every time.

Every task should prompt you to ask three questions:

- What do I need to know?
- What do I need to have?
- What do I need to do?

What Do I Need to *Know?*

What information do I need to satisfy my promise on time, every time, exactly as promised? In order to recognize what you need to know, you must understand the expectations of others, including your patients, your associates, and other employees. Are you clear on those expectations? Don't make the mistake of assuming you know. Instead, create a need-to-know checklist to make sure you ask all the necessary questions.

A need-to-know checklist might look like this:

- What are the expectations of my patients?
- What are the expectations of my administrators?
- What are the expectations of my associate chiropractors?
- What are the expectations of my staff?

What Do I Need to *Have?*

This question raises the issue of resources—namely, money, people, and time. If you don't have enough money to finance operations, how can you fulfill those expectations without creating cash-flow problems? If you don't have enough trained people, what happens then? And if you don't have enough time to manage your practice, what happens when you can't be in two places at once?

Don't assume that you can get what you need when you need it. Most often, you can't. And even if you can get what you need at the last minute, you'll pay dearly for it.

What Do I Need to *Do?*

The focus here is on actions to be started and finished. What do I need to do to fulfill the expectations of this patient on time, every time, exactly as promised? For example, what exactly are the steps to perform when seeing someone with spinal problems and related health conditions, or when designing the right care plan?

Your patients fall into distinct categories, and those categories make up your practice. The best chiropractic practices will invariably focus on fewer and fewer categories as they discover the importance of doing one thing better than anyone else.

Answering the question *What do I need to do?* demands a series of action plans, including

- the objective to be achieved;
- the standards by which you will know that the objective has been achieved;
- the benchmarks you need to reach in order for the objective to be achieved;
- the function/person accountable for the completion of the benchmarks;
- the budget for the completion of each benchmark; and
- the time by which each benchmark must be completed.

Your action plans should become the foundation for the completion plan. And the reason you need completion plans is to ensure that everything you do is not only realistic but can also be managed.

The Completion Plan

If the practice plan gives you results and provides you with standards, the completion plan tells you everything you need to know about every benchmark in the practice plan—that is, how you're going to fulfill patient expectations on time, every time, as promised. In other words, how you're going to arrange a referral to another professional, conduct routine adjustments, issue a recommendation for physical therapy, or educate a patient about her scoliosis.

The completion plan is essentially the operations manual, providing information about the details of doing tactical work. It is a guide to tell the people responsible for doing that work exactly how to do it.

Every completion plan becomes a part of the knowledge base of your business. No completion plan goes to waste. Every completion plan becomes a kind of textbook that explains to new employees or new associates joining your team how your practice operates in a way that distinguishes it from all other chiropractic practices.

To return to an earlier example, the completion plan for making a Big Mac is explicitly described in the *McDonald's Operation Manual*, as is every completion plan needed to run a McDonald's business.

The completion plan for a chiropractor might include the step-by-step details of how to analyze the physiological aspects of a patient's spine using the best clinical practice evidence—in contrast to how everyone else has learned to do it. Of course, every doctor of chiropractic has been taught X-ray analysis and a dozen other methods to analyze the spine. They've learned to do it the same way everyone else has learned to do it. But if you are going to stand out as unique in the minds of your patients, employees, and others, you must invent your own way of doing even ordinary things. Most of that value-added perception will come from your communication skills, your listening skills, your innovative skills in transforming an ordinary visit into a patient experience.

Perhaps you'll decide that a mandatory part of your surface electromyography procedure is to print out the completed study and show it to the patient, explaining what the different colors and numbers mean so that she has a better understanding of her own spine and nervous system. If no other chiropractor your patient has seen has ever taken the time to explain the procedure, you'll immediately set yourself apart. You must constantly raise the questions: *How do we do it here? How should we do it here?*

The quality of your answers will determine how effectively you distinguish your practice from every other chiropractor's practice.

Benchmarks

You can measure the movement of your practice—from what it is today to what it will be in the future—using business benchmarks. These are the goals you want your business to achieve during its lifetime.

Your benchmarks should include the following:

- Financial benchmarks
- Emotional benchmarks (the impact your practice will have on everyone who comes into contact with it)
- Performance benchmarks
- Patient benchmarks (Who are they? Why do they come to you? What does your practice give them that no one else does?)
- Employee benchmarks (How do you grow people? How do you find people who want to grow? How do you create a school in your practice that will teach your people skills they can't learn anywhere else?)

Your business benchmarks will reflect (1) the position your practice will hold in the minds and hearts of your patients, employees, and investors; and (2) how you intend to make that position a reality through the systems you develop.

Your benchmarks will describe how your management team will take shape and what systems you will need to develop so that your managers, just like McDonald's managers, will be able to produce the results for which they will be held accountable.

Benefits of the Planning Triangle

By implementing the Planning Triangle, you will discover

- what your practice will look, act, and feel like when it's fully evolved;
- when that's going to happen;

- how much money you will make; and
- much, much more.

These, then, are the primary purposes of the three critical plans: (1) to clarify precisely what needs to be done to get what the chiropractor wants from his or her practice and life, and (2) to define the specific steps by which it will happen.

First *this* must happen, then *that* must happen. One, two, three. By monitoring your progress, step by step, you can determine whether you're on the right track.

That's what planning is all about. It's about creating a standard—a yardstick—against which you will be able to measure your performance.

Failing to create such a standard is like throwing a straw into a hurricane. Who knows where that straw will land?

Have you taken the leap? Have you accepted that the word *business* and the word *practice* are not synonymous? That a practice relies on the chiropractor and a business relies on other people plus a system?

Because most chiropractors are control freaks, 99 percent of today's chiropractic companies are practices, not businesses.

The result, as a friend of mine says, is that "chiropractors are spending all day stamping out fires when all around them the forest is ablaze. They're out of touch, and that chiropractor better take control of the practice before someone else does."

Because chiropractors are never taught to think like businesspeople, the health-care professional is forever at war with the businessperson. This is especially evident in large, multidiscipline practices, where bureaucrats (businesspeople) often try to control chiropractors (health-care professionals). They usually end up treating each other as combatants. In fact, the single greatest reason chiropractors become entrepreneurs is to divorce such bureaucrats and to begin to reinvent the chiropractic enterprise.

That's you. Now the divorce is over and a new love affair has begun. You're a chiropractor with a plan! Who wouldn't want to do business with such a person?

Now let's take the next step in our strategic odyssey. Let's take a closer look at the subject of *management*. But before we do, let's listen to what Dr. Frank has to say about planning.✤

> To find out exactly what your three critical plans will look like when they're finished, go to www.michaelegerber.com/co-author.

CHAPTER 6

Make Plans—Your Future is Closer Than It Looks

Dr. Frank Sovinsky

Planning is bringing the future into the present so that you can do something about it now.

—Alan Lakein

You no doubt felt something as you read that last chapter. I know I did. Did you feel a sense of awe, like, "Ahhh, there it is. That's what I have been missing!" or a sense of regret, like, "Aw, I wish I had done this sooner."

Did you feel a bit overwhelmed by the scale of organization that it takes to be truly successful? Or did a little voice say, "Oh great, goal setting. This stuff never works for me." That's the most common reaction I hear, and I can understand why you might feel that way. What I promise is a fresh look at a misunderstood process that I know will work for you.

Planning is bringing your dreams and desires from the future into the present, so that they can be touched, molded, and worked. Do you realize how extraordinary that is? As an entrepreneur you

51

have a say in your future, but it will not be handed to you. There is no need to echo Michael's words of wisdom from the last chapter. What I intend to do is to highlight the process that you will need to engage in as a chiropractic entrepreneur.

The good news is that you now have a guide and, well, a plan for how to plan. This disciplined, methodical approach will open your mind to the possibilities for your business and then organize the pieces for action.

The genius of the Planning Triangle is that it makes a difficult process organic. Trust me, I am not moved by painstaking tasks and details, and that's why this process works. It has a hierarchy where one thing follows the next. Start it and you will see what I mean. It will wake you up at night, get you up early, and call to you from the mountain. Answer this call. You will thank yourself later.

As the owner of your practice, it is your vision, planning, and management that will shape its destiny. We have important work to do, and I don't want these foundational platforms to be built on a fault line, or to be ignored because you are too busy trying to keep up with your practice's demands.

So here's the first step: Continue to read, and when you are finished for the day, I want you to go online and book a "business vision trip." Plan on a two- or three-day quest, and choose a place that boosts your mental concentration and eliminates distractions. No golfing, no skiing, no recreation just yet. Because this is strategic work, you need to get the entrepreneur, the chiropractor-as-owner, awake and ready to help you with the Planning Triangle. The employee is not invited!

Choose an environment that is quiet and stress-free. A nice hotel in natural surroundings works for me, and at other times I go to a luxury hotel in the city. You need time to write your thoughts down on paper or in your computer. Unless it is written, it doesn't exist anywhere other than in your head.

This is important personal work, and you may choose to be alone during this business quest. I choose to take my wife with me because we bring different strengths to the strategic process. It makes the tactical work a whole lot easier to implement once we get home because she was there in that creative moment.

Listen closely. Your new mantra is "Today, not tomorrow!" Stop getting ready to get ready. Book it. It may be a couple of weeks or more until you can make the trip, so be here now. Keep reading and working on your business, and when you get to your retreat, you will have seed ideas to plant and nourish.

Let It Flow

Now it's time to fully engage that three pounds of gelatinous mass between your ears. Unleash the power of your thoughts. Your mind is naturally creative, and it is a perfect problem-solver if given the right direction and environment. So I want you to take a blank sheet of paper and draw the Planning Triangle on it. Make it large and colorful. You will want to jot down a few ideas or draw a few images as you read this chapter. You might even want to get an artist's drawing tablet as your ideas spread out and onto a mind map.

A mind map is a nonlinear approach to note taking and gives you room to explore an idea with symbols and drawings. For more information, search online and you will discover software to assist you in mind mapping, yet a simple drawing pad gets it done for me. Have some fun even if you can only draw stick people like I do. If you prefer to use the linear outline model, go for it. What matters is that it gets done.

Your Business Plan—Who You Are

The business plan wants you to answer this question: What will your business look like when it grows up? Seems like a pretty straightforward question, doesn't it? Yet the right answer for you may not come as cleanly and swiftly as you imagine. And I am willing to bet that it will change as you continue to use the processes in this book. Stay open. The practice you have right now will not be the same one that carries you across the "equity goal line."

The story of your practice is the story of the people you serve and how your practice does it better than anyone else's. This story needs to be conveyed in such a way that it inspires you, your staff, your patients, your business alliances, and everyone within your circle of influence. Make no mistake. This is not the common "mission statement" that hangs on your wall. This story lives in your chiropractic soul. As it comes to you, write it down in a conversational tone, not as an essay or "chiro-speak."

I really want to know about you, about what you do, and why it matters. Imagine that we are sitting in a cafe, adequately caffeinated, and I am talking at 150 words per minute with bursts up to 250. Answer these questions as they come. Doctor, what is the purpose of your business? What problem are you solving? How will you solve it? Who will help you provide these solutions? Go ahead and answer aloud, I want to hear you. Then write your answers down on the Planning Triangle or mind map.

Your answers must be more specific than, "To help people live healthier lives." What people? Where do they come from? What do they want from you? What services will you be able to provide and still make a profit? Get the idea?

Your Vision

The number one problem with most business plans is that that the chiropractor designs a practice around the products and services that he or she likes. This creates a doctor-centered business and limits the practice to a handful of fans. Passion is important, yet you have to ask yourself two questions: "Other than me and the patients I have right now, who else really cares about this?" and "Who else will be willing to trade their time and their money for this thing I do?"

The "who else" in business lexicon is your target market, the people you want to attract to your business. Do your research and find the data points that will help you answer the following questions:

Is there sufficient real-world interest in what I do? What can I do better than any other business in my community that promises health-care solutions?

You have had enough experience in life to realize just how impressionable our minds are to outside influences. I am telling you this because the business plan must have your vision, not someone else's. Let's assume for a moment that the vision or image that you have in your head right now is not entirely yours. That's just my opinion, and what if I am right? If I am right, you will be wasting time, money, and effort working very hard on the things that will never work for you.

Some of you were influenced by a benevolent chiropractor who touched your life in a profound way. You might have been so affected that you may think your key to success is to replicate that chiropractor's practice model. It may be true, but it still needs to be your vision.

Most of us are influenced by our trade journals, colleagues, and the seminars we attend. While it is important to see other perspectives and to share ideas, too often the messages are mixed and incomplete. As a result, most doctors end up with analysis paralysis and never take action. You not only need an action plan, you have to act on your plan. This E-Myth path is congruent, complete, and, most important, effective. Your search is over.

Your Practice Plan—What You Do

As we write this book, health-care reform policies have changed. Whether it is reformed or not remains to be seen. I mention it because it should be a wake-up call that policies outside your control should never affect your results. That's right, your plan and execution of that plan must be a standard for clinical excellence, and a consistent financial performer regardless of the economy or government mandates.

The future is already here, and those who are thriving provide affordable, accessible, and hassle-free chiropractic care. With appropriate overhead and adequate patient volume, your care plan can be affordable to most seeking your help.

With tightly orchestrated systems, patients can get the care they want and have access to that care during patient-preferred times. And with a clear understanding of psychographics, your patients will receive hassle-free care.

A patient-centered practice model makes the decision process simple for the patient. The financial and clinical recommendations are straightforward. The clinical recommendations are individualized according to the findings, not a cookie-cutter method. Patient-centered care promotes physical, emotional, and financial independence.

One thing I know is this: Chiropractors don't always agree about clinical protocols, techniques, or care plans. Yet I think most of us will agree that our examination, diagnosis, and treatment solutions need to blend the best available research, our clinical experience, and the patient's preference.

While the focal point is the relationship between the spine and the nervous system, we investigate and inform our patients about other strategies that they may need. This creates a health-care mentoring relationship and gives the patient responsibilities and more choices. Now back to the E-Myth perspective and what you need to do with the business model you choose.

You can have a patient-centric approach with slight variances in your business model. Just for clarity, a business model is the way your business makes money. You may choose to provide chiropractic care as your core service and serve as a gatekeeper, or what I call a "patient concierge," when other strategies are necessary. Or you may decide to provide chiropractic care along with complementary services and health-related products all under one roof. If you decide on this direction, you will need a process and a system to support each service, and highly motivated, skilled chiropractic technicians to use those systems.

If you already have a practice that offers a variety of products and services like massage, nutritional advice, and products and rehabilitation, each profit center needs to be assessed for its relative profit margins and its contribution to the practice's bottom line. You can't just say, "I purchase glucosamine for $7.50 a bottle and sell it for $15, so my profit is $7.50." Here's why.

There are two types of revenue. The first source is passive income, which is interest and capital derived from investments. The second source of revenue is active income. It is all the money produced directly by your business, and it requires someone to do something.

Each of the services you provide, whether it is an exam, adjustment, therapy, or product, is a result of someone's labor. Some may consider supplements and orthopedic supports passive income, and they are mistaken because it still requires someone to do something in exchange for that money. Someone has to order, stock, display, and sell them. Therefore, it is active income. Keep in mind that stocked items have a shelf life and will end up in the trash, and that rows of supplements freeze the flow of money.

When I talk to doctors about the other services they provide and the profit they generate, I hear comments like, "The massage therapist charges $45 and I get $25, so my profit is $25; it's a great deal." This does not meet the criteria for a sound understanding of profit. You must factor in overhead (heating, lighting, etc.), and what about the use of your staff for booking patients and collecting fees? You need to look closely to determine if the room you are using for massage could make more per hour as an adjusting room or additional exam room. One question will lead to another, and your uncommon, relentless pursuit will bring your vision into focus.

The Practice Plan—What You Do

The chiropractic services that you provide are only one piece of the impact your business has on the patients and their personal community of family and friends. As an example, you may have incredible clinical skills that produce amazing results, yet because your financial systems are inadequate or confusing, your business fails to grow. On the other hand, you may have incredible financial systems, yet as a result of mediocre exam procedures, your business fails to grow. And, of course, you may have great clinical competencies and solid financial systems, yet as a result of a poorly trained or motivated staff, your business fails to grow.

The E-Myth solution is to organize the work that needs to get done. That's where systems and procedures fit in. They are the documents that answer the questions: What are the expectations? What is our standard of care, performance, and service for every task we do in our office? Who does what, when, where, why, and exactly how in order to meet and surpass those expectations? They are the "ownership manuals" for each and every employee's position. They are used for training as well as directions to refer to instead of asking for help.

High performance requires high standards. Explicit, well-conceived standards help people know exactly what's expected of them and make it much more likely that you will get the results you want. You will recruit, hire, and develop motivated people, who are inspired by the story of your practice, to implement these systems. So that our lexicon is in order, this is how we see it.

A *procedure* is a specific instruction or a series of steps to be followed by an individual to arrive at a desired outcome. This is often called "Standard Operating Procedure" (SOP).

Systems are how the whole team comes together to deliver a service. A new patient system includes procedures for the front tech, the exam tech, the financial tech, and the doctor that, when all integrated, result in a remarkable experience for the new patient.

The Completion Plan—How You Do It

The liberation of your practice is truly completed when you have created a handbook for new and existing employees to refer to. We recommend you develop an action plan for each system that clearly illustrates each person's duties in the system. Include a brief description of the procedure and who will be accountable for it.

This guidebook needs to include

- the story of your business;
- the systems documentation and staff accountability;
- the step-by-step procedures; and
- the training resources.

Once you have this documented, all you will need to do is to review and update it every six months. And even that review becomes systematized. Procedures are ever-changing. They can be tweaked, completely overhauled, or deleted and replaced. But while they are in effect, they provide a common, unspoken denominator that allows highest efficiency and satisfaction to govern.

Developing and documenting your systems and procedures will result in happier patients, more satisfied employees, increased profits, and better patient-centered care.

There is no "right" format for your procedure manual. It can assume whatever style you choose. Whether you want to begin with numbers or letters, use diagrams or lists, graphics or text, capital letters, bold type, or underlines, it's your choice. However you choose to format your manual, just get it done.

Small Business, Big Responsibility

The business of chiropractic is composed of three distinct departments, the Clinical Department, the Financial Department, and the Human Resources Department. Each department is defined by its systems and procedures to ensure a predictable service experience for the patient.

Together these departments guide and support the chiropractic tech and the doctor by eliminating confusion surrounding the many variables that a bustling practice encounters. These departments support one another and contribute equally to the orchestration of a world-class chiropractic office.

The Clinical Department

The Clinical Department is responsible for all patient-care activities. Direct patient care includes performing the appropriate exam segments, adjunctive care procedures, and patient instruction. The Clinical Department is responsible for documenting outcome assessments, keeping patient case histories, coordinating outside diagnostics, and acquiring records from other health-care providers as required.

All "patient scheduling" systems fall within this department's responsibilities, including making appointments for office visits, new patient exams, and established patient re-exams; completing patient reports; and rescheduling missed appointments.

DC Mentors' Practice Management Program suggests that the Clinical Department systems look something like this:

- New Patient Clinical System
- Report of Findings System
- Established Patient System
- Interim Exam System
- Patient Instruction System (ergonomics, nutrition, home therapies)
- Missed Appointment System
- Adjunctive Care System, e.g. Massage Therapist System (consistent technique, massage oils, aromatherapy, lighting, music, tables, sheets, time with client, and fee)

Take each additional service you provide and make a manual of your standards and point-by-point instruction.

The Financial Department

The Financial Department is responsible for all the financial activities. This includes insurance company communications, relating and enforcing financial policies, billing, at-the-counter collections, maintaining statistics, and other accounting activities.

DC Mentors suggests the following Financial Department systems:

- Statistical Management System
- New Patient Financial System
- Collections Systems (front desk collection, billing)
- Accounts Payable System
- Overhead Assessment System
- Daily Accounting
- Practice Marketing System

The Human Resources Department

The Human Resources Department is responsible for recruiting, hiring, training, and developing the people in the practice. This process is ongoing and includes training the soft skills as well as the tactical work for each position in the practice.

DC Mentors suggests the following Human Resources Department systems:

- Recruiting, Hiring System
- Chiropractic Tech Development and Accountability System
- Associate Chiropractor Development and Accountability System
- Team-building System

Along with undercapitalization, unrealistic expectations concerning practice growth smother doctors in a blanket of confusion, frustration, and self-doubt. Overnight success takes, on average, seven years to manifest. I know many of you are talented and driven, and are optimistic that you can prove me wrong. I hope you do! Yet a solid completion plan, with a realistic timeline for achieving your benchmarks, will give you the space you need to create the processes and embody the E-Myth principles.

There is hope when there is a plan. Are you feeling that sense of urgency again? Now that your plan is coming together, we need to hear what Michael has to say about management. ✤

CHAPTER 7

On the Subject of Management

Michael E. Gerber

Good management consists of showing average people how to do the work of superior people.

—John D. Rockefeller

Every chiropractor, including Steve, eventually faces the issues of management. Most face it badly.

Why do so many chiropractors suffer from a kind of paralysis when it comes to dealing with management? Why are so few able to get their chiropractic practice to work the way they want it to and to run it on time? Why are their managers (if they have any) seemingly so inept?

There are two main problems. First, the chiropractor usually abdicates accountability for management by hiring an office manager. Thus, the chiropractor is working hand in glove with someone who is supposed to do the managing. But the chiropractor is unmanageable himself!

The chiropractor doesn't think like a manager because he doesn't think he is a manager. He's a chiropractor! He rules the roost. And so he gets the office manager to take care of stuff like scheduling appointments, keeping his calendar, collecting receivables, hiring/firing, and much more.

Second, no matter who does the managing, they usually have a completely dysfunctional idea of what it means to manage. They're trying to manage people, contrary to what is needed.

We often hear that a good manager must be a "people person." Someone who loves to nourish, figure out, support, care for, teach, baby, monitor, mentor, direct, track, motivate, and, if all else fails, threaten or beat up her people.

Don't believe it. Management has far less to do with people than you've been led to believe.

In fact, despite the claims of every management book written by management gurus (who have seldom managed anything), no one—with the exception of a few bloodthirsty tyrants—has ever learned how to manage people.

And the reason is simple: *People are almost impossible to manage*.

Yes, it's true. People are unmanageable. They're inconsistent, unpredictable, unchangeable, unrepentant, irrepressible, and generally impossible.

Doesn't knowing this make you feel better? Now you understand why you've had all those problems! Do you feel the relief, the heavy stone lifted from your chest?

The time has come to fully understand what management is really all about. Rather than managing *people*, management is really all about managing a *process*, a step-by-step way of doing things, which, combined with other processes, becomes a system. For example:

- The process for on-time scheduling
- The process for answering the telephone
- The process for greeting a patient
- The process for organizing patient files

Thus, a process is the step-by-step way of doing something over time. Considered as a whole, these processes are a system:

- The on-time scheduling system
- The telephone answering system
- The patient greeting system
- The file organization system

Instead of managing people, then, the truly effective manager has been taught a system for managing a process through which people get things done.

More precisely, managers and their people, *together*, manage the processes—the systems—that comprise your business. Management is less about *who* gets things done in your business than about *how* things get done.

In fact, great managers are not fascinated with people, but with how things get done through people. Great managers are masters at figuring out how to get things done effectively and efficiently through people using extraordinary systems.

Great managers constantly ask key questions, such as:

- What is the result we intend to produce?
- Are we producing that result every single time?
- If we're not producing that result every single time, why not?
- If we are producing that result every single time, how could we produce even better results?
- Do we lack a system? If so, what would that system look like if we were to create it?
- If we have a system, why aren't we using it?

And so forth.

In short, a great manager can leave the office fully assured that it will run at least as well as it does when he or she is physically in the room.

Great managers are those who use a great management system. A system that shouts, "This is *how* we manage here." Not "This is *who* manages here."

In a truly effective company, how you manage is always more important than who manages. Provided a system is in place, how you manage is transferable, whereas who manages isn't. *How* you manage can be taught, whereas *who* manages can't be.

When a company is dependent on *who* manages—Katie, Kim, or Kevin—that business is in serious jeopardy. Because when Katie, Kim, or Kevin leaves, that business has to start over again. What an enormous waste of time and resources!

Even worse, when a company is dependent on *who* manages, you can bet all the managers in that business are doing their own thing. What could be more unproductive than ten managers who each manage in a unique way? How in the world could you possibly manage those managers?

The answer is: You can't. Because it takes you right back to trying to manage *people* again.

And, as I hope you now know, that's impossible.

In this chapter, I often refer to managers in the plural. I know that most chiropractors only have one manager—the office manager. And so you may be thinking that a management system isn't so important in a small chiropractic practice. After all, the office manager does whatever an office manager does (and thank God, because you don't want to do it).

But if your practice is ever going to turn into the business it could become, and if that business is ever going to turn into the enterprise of your dreams, then the questions you ask about how the office manager manages your affairs are critical ones. Because until you come to grips with your dual role as owner and key employee, and the relationship your manager has to those two roles, your practice/business/enterprise will never realize its potential. Thus the need for a management system.

Management System

What, then, is a management system?

The E-Myth says that a management system is the method by which every manager innovates, quantifies, orchestrates, and then monitors the systems through which your practice produces the results you expect.

According to the E-Myth, a manager's job is simple:

A manager's job is to invent the systems through which the owner's vision is consistently and faithfully manifested at the operating level of the business.

Which brings us right back to the purpose of your business and the need for an entrepreneurial vision.

Are you beginning to see what I'm trying to share with you? That your business is one single thing? And that all the subjects we're discussing here—money, planning, management, and so on— are all about doing one thing well?

That one thing is the one thing your practice is intended to do: distinguish your chiropractic business from all others.

It is the manager's role to make certain it all fits. And it's your role as entrepreneur to make sure your manager knows what the business is supposed to look, act, and feel like when it's finally done. As clearly as you know how, you must convey to your manager what you know to be true—your vision, your picture of the business when it's finally done. In this way, your vision is translated into your manager's marching orders every day he or she reports to work.

Unless that vision is embraced by your manager, you and your people will suffer from the tyranny of routine. And your business will suffer from it, too.

Now let's move on to *people*. Because, as we know, it's people who are causing all our problems. But before we do, let's hear what Dr. Frank has to say about management. ✤

CHAPTER

8

Management by Design

Dr. Frank Sovinsky

Management is efficiency in climbing the ladder of success; leadership determines whether the ladder is leaning against the right wall.

—Stephen R. Covey

Are you beginning to see how the E-Myth view of management is going to set you free? Can you feel the relief just knowing that someday soon you will no longer need to "herd cats?" Truth is, herding cats is easier than trying to manage people.

If you're like most chiropractors, as your practice grew so did the rest of the business hassles and details. To keep it going, you needed to find help. So you gave a staff member the title "office manager" and the command, "Here, you do this, I am too busy adjusting patients."

Assigning tasks that you don't know how to do or don't want to do is the path of least resistance, and it is full of potholes.

To achieve the results you want, you will need to have a conversation with the real manager of this practice, you. And you will need to cultivate a manager's mindset and create the systems that the manager can use to innovate, quantify, and orchestrate the practice.

As a chiropractor, you are very adept at seeing the big picture. You see things others rarely notice. You recognize that local health conditions have a global effect, and that global conditions have a local effect. Use those critical-thinking skills to heal your practice.

First, I want to make certain that you are focused on what it is you are doing right here, right now. Say the title of this book out loud, *The E-Myth Chiropractor: Why Most Chiropractic Practices Don't Work and What to Do About It*. What does that mean to you? I have asked this question of hundreds of doctors, and no one to date has been able to give me a complete answer.

I know you are intelligent, yet sometimes the simple things are the most profound. If you answered, "Most chiropractic practices don't work, therefore the chiropractor is stuck doing all the work the practice should be doing," then you nailed it. Congratulations.

Now back to what to do about it. Your first step is to stop managing your people and shift your complete attention to managing the work that your practice needs to get done. This magnificent construct of managing the work, not the people, frees you and your staff from becoming trapped in a personality-controlled practice. It sets the stage for a purpose-driven practice.

Together we will show you how to create the tools that you, the practice's manager, need to have in order to monitor how your practice is performing in real time.

Manage the Work and Then Lead Your People

As the manager of your business, you have the structural authority and obligation to be rigorous as you monitor the standards of your practice and your staff's performance. As the manager, you will need to separate performance objectives and standards from the person.

As an example, you may have a really great person who can't do what the job requires. What do you do? Do you create a job just for that person? Do you move the person to another position and hope he or she can handle it? The manager sees it differently. The manager asks, "What does the practice need?"

The initial consultation with a potential client of DC Mentors begins with a Business Needs Analysis, which includes a review of statistics, staff performance, and getting a clear picture of the doctor's vision for his or her practice. Yet the discussion is most often bogged down with staff issues and the excuses doctors make for keeping poor performers or even people who have bad attitudes.

Here are a few of my favorites. "I can't let Isabella go because she is the only one who knows the billing software." "Ethan has been with me a long time, and if I let him go, what will the patients think?" "Olivia was a patient I hired. She's been with me since I started. If I fire her, I'll lose her entire family." This soap opera is brought to you by a personality-controlled practice.

Staff infections are iatrogenic. That's right. You are the source and carrier of the poor-performance virus. So you need to develop a healthy psychological immune system in order to make the logical decisions that a manager would make.

When a practice isn't working, the numbers tell the story of a rudderless ship. Let me share a few behavioral signs that your practice lacks a management system.

At the top of the list are the weekly staff meetings where, when all is said and done, more is said than done. How about the chiropractor-as-employee who shares his or her frustration with declining numbers and income and asks fellow employees for advice: "If this were your practice, what would you do?"

Another more devastating behavioral sign of a lack of management is insubordination. Insubordination can wipe a practice off the face of the community. It can be a silent roll of the eyes when you ask a tech to do something, or be as piercing as the absolute refusal to implement a change. The manager should never tolerate it, and with a management system in place, you will prevent it from ever happening.

Know It, Document It, and Then Delegate It

If you don't comprehend every part of every position in your office, you are being held hostage somewhere. This doesn't mean you should perform every position, but you should know how you want it performed.

This is a great reason to get to know the work of each position and have the techs help you document exactly what it is they do. Then you can compare and contrast "how the work is done now" against your business plan and "how the work needs to be done" from this point forward.

Now that you have decided to begin the process of documenting your performance expectations, you must set the tone or the work may never get done. If your staff thinks the manual is just a bunch of words designed to "keep them in line," it probably won't get written. If they think writing out procedures is just busy work, or respond with something like, "Why should I do that? I already know what needs to be done," nothing will change.

A great place to begin is to say, "I have made a decision. We are going to construct a guidebook of policies, procedures, and account-abilities. This will make certain that our patients get the quality of care they have come to expect of us." Then shut up and delegate the work.

Do not build your systems and procedures around your current people. Just because your current front tech, Chloe, is "better" at something than the exam tech, Jacob, or because it has always been done a certain way, or Hannah is the only one who knows how to do it, do not let that dictate the way it will be done and who will do it from now on. To get to your next level, you need to create all of your systems and procedures without personalities involved.

I hope you have the right people who are able and willing to do what needs to be done. If you don't, my dear manager, then you have a decision to make.

Role Awareness

According to the E-Myth design, "A manager's job is to invent the systems through which the owner's vision is consistently and faithfully manifested at the operating level of the business."

Most chiropractors are hostages in their own practices because they abdicate important managerial tasks to a staff member and then become dependent on a personality rather than a reproducible system. The ordinary practice has an office manager who is, in most cases, a talented and loyal employee. This staff member likely earned his or her way with hard work and probably tenure. However, there is a problem with this arrangement. By definition, most office managers do not meet the criterion for the position of manager.

The extraordinary practice can pull this crucial lynchpin and unlock sustainable growth in three ways.

You can recruit and hire someone who has experience in creating systems and can quantify the results and orchestrate the work of the practice through documentation and monitoring of the systems. Your recruitment efforts will be focused upon finding a person who can do both strategic and tactical work for your vision. That person's skill set needs to be loaded, and he or she will need to be adequately compensated. The economic reality is that most offices in the infancy and adolescent stage cannot afford to hire this person.

The second option is to outsource this work and hire a practice management company. This is where hype gets a reality check. Be diligent in your search. We all need a little inspiration in our lives and a sense of community. But you need more than a pep rally before the game. You have what I call a "business matured" perspective. Chapter by chapter you are gaining perspective. You are growing in your appreciation of exactly what it will take to build your community's best practice. You need substance, not sizzle. A client-centered practice management company will listen to your vision, the story of your practice, and plug in the appropriate systems and processes. It will then teach you how to be the manager so that you know how to quantify and navigate the terrain of practice development.

The third option is to do it yourself, to embrace the role of manager, and get it done. Even if you choose to outsource and hire a coaching company, you will want to go through this process. Own it and it will be a skill that lasts a lifetime.

Keeping Score

You can't manage what you can't see or refuse to see. The E-Myth attitude embodies an important attribute that no other book on business addresses: the eloquent and honest notion that your business is a game, and that your responsibility is to make it a game worth playing for you and your team. Notice that I said the *business* of chiropractic is a game. Caring for your patients is, of course, a sacred trust.

Games are much more fun to play when you keep score. Imagine playing tennis without a net, basketball without a rim, or football without an end zone. Keeping score is benchmarking, and it can be fun with the right attitude.

The scorecard for your practice is the Statistical Management System. When you approach statistics with this attitude, the spreadsheet takes on a whole new level of enrollment. With accurate statistics, you can evaluate the practice and make key decisions and adjustments to the game's strategy. A wining one!

I wish I had read this book. Because I remember the day I felt like I had a cash-flow problem—well, let's just say I noticed I had no cash. I looked around after the patients and staff were gone for the day and found a drawer full of unbilled patient routing slips! If I had been tracking my financial department's collection statistic, the situation would never have gotten so dire. I, the manager, didn't give the staff a system and procedures to follow, and I didn't have a system for monitoring. It was a costly mistake.

Integrity is doing what you say you will do. Statistics and performance reviews keep you and your entire staff accountable to the vision of the practice. It helps create a "culture of accountability."

The Statistical Management System is designed for you to review your data points, and in doing so maintain a head-on and hands-on style of leadership behavior. You should review the numbers weekly to keep your fingers on the pulse of the practice, and study them with a deeper, more critical eye every three months.

We have seen many struggling doctors demonstrate the signs and symptoms of SOCD, statistical obsessive compulsive disorder. SOCD behavior comes in two styles.

The **numbers stalker** who unconsciously or consciously counts patients throughout the day.

The **numbers dodger** who refuses to monitor and mark progress because of the emotional pain he or she associates with the business.

Both forms of SOCD imprison the doctor, causing needless suffering. The unsettling fact is that a doctor who consciously feeds SOCD engages in this behavior because it gives a sense of control.

Another common statistical behavior is the SADD doctor, statistical attention deficit disorder. The SADD doctor keeps statistics and may glance at them occasionally but never takes the time to look at them critically. Consequently, the doctor makes changes in the practice but never stops to look at the effects or consequences those changes had on the business.

If you take charge of your practice, you won't need to control it. As your managerial and leadership skills develop, you will lose the need to control. Control takes two forms: the manager who abdicates the responsibilities, and the micromanager who never lets go.

The way to create lasting solutions is to see all of your business challenges as a consequence—the end result of nonexistent, poorly developed, dated, or inadequate systems. Developing systemic thinking enables you to clearly see whether there are any commonalities in your frustrations. You might discover that poor performance issues all happen in the same system (New Patient Attraction, Patient Compliance, and Patient Fulfillment) or department (Clinical,

Financial, and Human Resources). Armed with this analysis you can then identify, analyze, and isolate the common elements and make the necessary corrections.

Congratulations; you covered a lot of ground in the last eight chapters. Keep that mind of yours wide open, because the hits just keep coming as Michael teaches us about people in the next chapter. ✤

9

On the Subject of People

Michael E. Gerber

Very few people go to the doctor when they have a cold. They go to the theatre instead.

—Oscar Wilde

E very chiropractor I've ever met has complained about people.
About employees: "They come in late, they go home early, they have the focus of an antique camera!"

About insurance companies: "They're living in a nonparallel universe!"

About patients: "They want me to repair thirty years of bad habits and inadequate spinal care!"

People, people, people. Every chiropractor's nemesis. And at the heart of it all are the people who work for you.

"By the time I tell them how to do it, I could have done it twenty times myself!" "How come nobody listens to what I say?" "Why is it nobody ever does what I ask them to do?" Does this sound like you?

So what's the problem with people? To answer that, think back to the last time you walked into a chiropractor's office. What did you see in the people's faces?

Most people working in chiropractic are harried. You can see it in their expressions. They're negative. They're bad-spirited. They're humorless. And with good reason. After all, they're surrounded by people who have headaches, or are suffering from sciatica, or—worst-case scenario—may even be a candidate for spinal surgery. Patients are looking for nurturing, for empathy, for care. And many are either terrified or depressed. They don't want to be there.

Is it any wonder employees at most chiropractic practices are disgruntled? They're surrounded by unhappy people all day. They're answering the same questions 24/7. And most of the time, the chiropractor has no time for them. He or she is too busy leading a dysfunctional life.

Working with people brings great joy—and monumental frustration. And so it is with chiropractors and their people. But why? And what can we do about it?

Let's look at the typical chiropractor—who this person is and isn't.

Most chiropractors are unprepared to use other people to get results. Not because they can't find people, but because they are fixated on getting the results themselves. In other words, most chiropractors are not the businesspeople they need to be, but *technicians suffering from an entrepreneurial seizure.*

Am I talking about you? What were you doing before you became an entrepreneur?

Were you an associate chiropractor working for a large multi-clinic organization? A midsized practice? A small practice?

Didn't you imagine owning your own practice as the way out?

Didn't you think that because you knew how to do the technical work—because you knew so much about sports injuries, spinal correction, and wellness—that you were automatically prepared to create a practice that does that type of work?

Didn't you figure that by creating your own practice, you could dump the boss once and for all? How else to get rid of that impossible person, the one driving you crazy, the one who never let you do your own thing, the one who was the main reason you decided to take the leap into a business of your own in the first place?

Didn't you start your own practice so that you could become your own boss?

And didn't you imagine that once you became your own boss, you would be free to do whatever you wanted to do—and to take home *all* the money?

Honestly, isn't that what you imagined? So you went into business for yourself and immediately dived into work.

Doing it, doing it, doing it.

Busy, busy, busy.

Until one day you realized (or maybe not) that you were doing all of the work. You were doing everything you knew how to do, plus a lot more you knew nothing about. Building sweat equity, you thought.

In reality, a technician suffering from an entrepreneurial seizure.

You were just hoping to make a buck in your own practice. And sometimes you did earn a wage. But other times you didn't. You were the one signing the checks, all right, but they went to other people.

Does this sound familiar? Is it driving you crazy?

Well, relax, because we're going to show you the right way to do it this time.

Read carefully. Be mindful of the moment. You are about to learn the secret you've been waiting for all your working life.

The People Law

It's critical to know this about the working life of chiropractors who own their own chiropractic practice: *Without people, you don't own a practice, you own a job.* And it can be the worst job in the world because you're working for a lunatic! (Nothing personal—but we've got to face facts.)

Let me state what every chiropractor knows: Without people, you're going to have to do it all yourself. Without human help, you're doomed to try to do too much. This isn't a breakthrough idea, but it's amazing how many chiropractors ignore the truth. They end up knocking themselves out, ten to twelve hours a day. They try to do more, but less actually gets done.

The load can double you over and leave you panting. In addition to the work you're used to doing, you may also have to do the books. And the organizing. And the filing. You'll have to do the planning and the scheduling. When you own your own practice, the daily minutiae are never-ceasing—as I'm sure you've found out. Like painting the Golden Gate Bridge, it's endless. Which puts it beyond the realm of human possibility. Until you discover how to get it done by somebody else, it will continue on and on until you're a burned-out husk.

But with others helping you, things will start to drastically improve. If, that is, you truly understand how to engage people in the work you need them to do. When you learn how to do that, when you learn how to replace yourself with other people—people trained in your system—then your practice can really begin to grow. Only then will you begin to experience true freedom yourself.

What typically happens is that chiropractors, knowing they need help answering the phone, filing, and so on, go out and find people who can do these things. Once they delegate these duties, however, they rarely spend any time with the employee. Deep down they feel it's not important *how* these things get done; it's only important that they get done.

They fail to grasp the requirement for a system that makes people their greatest asset rather than their greatest liability. A system so reliable that if Chris dropped dead tomorrow, Leslie could do exactly what Chris did. That's where the People Law comes in.

The People Law says that each time you add a new person to your practice using an intelligent (turnkey) system that works, you expand your reach. And you can expand your reach almost infinitely! People allow you to be everywhere you want to be simultaneously, without actually having to be there in the flesh.

People are to a chiropractor what a record was to Frank Sinatra. A Sinatra record could be (and still is) played in a million places at the same time, regardless of where Frank was. And every record sale produced royalties for Sinatra (or his estate).

With the help of other people, Sinatra created a quality recording that faithfully replicated his unique talents, then made sure it was marketed and distributed, and the revenue managed.

Your people can do the same thing for you. All *you* need to do is to create a "recording"—a system—of your unique talents, your special way of practicing chiropractic, and then replicate it, market it, distribute it, and manage the revenue.

Isn't that what successful businesspeople do? Make a "recording" of their most effective ways of doing business? In this way, they provide a turnkey solution to their patients' problems. A system solution that really works.

Doesn't your practice offer the same potential for you that records did for Sinatra (and now for his heirs)? The ability to produce income without having to go to work every day?

Isn't that what your people could be for you? The means by which your system for practicing chiropractic could be faithfully replicated?

But first you've got to have a system. You have to create a unique way of doing business that you can teach to your people, that you can manage faithfully, and that you can replicate consistently, just like McDonald's.

Because without such a system, without such a "recording," without a unique way of doing business that really works, all you're left with is people doing their own thing. And that is almost always a recipe for chaos. Rather than guaranteeing consistency, it encourages mistake after mistake after mistake.

And isn't that how the problem started in the first place? People doing whatever *they* perceived they needed to do, regardless of what you wanted? People left to their own devices, with no regard for the costs of their behavior? The costs to you?

In other words, people without a system.

Can you imagine what would have happened to Frank Sinatra if he had followed that example? If every one of his recordings had been done differently? Imagine a million different versions of "My Way." It's unthinkable.

Would you buy a record like that? What if Frank were having a bad day? What if he had a sore throat?

Please hear this: The People Law is unforgiving. Without a systematic way of doing business, people are more often a liability than an asset. Unless you prepare, you'll find out too late which ones are which.

The People Law says that without a specific system for doing business; without a specific system for recruiting, hiring, and training your people to use that system; and without a specific system for managing and improving your systems, your practice will always be a crapshoot.

Do you want to roll the dice with your practice at stake? Unfortunately, that is what most chiropractors are doing.

The People Law also says that you can't effectively delegate your responsibilities unless you have something specific to delegate. And that something specific is a way of doing business that works!

Frank Sinatra is gone, but his voice lives on. And someone is still counting his royalties. That's because Sinatra had a system that worked.

Do you? Let's see if Dr. Frank does, and then we will move on to the subject of associate chiropractors. ✤

CHAPTER 10

People Are Your Dream Team

Dr. Frank Sovinsky

Without a compelling cause, our employees are just putting in time. Their minds might be engaged, but their hearts are not.

—Lee J. Colan

Your practice makes a bold statement in your community. "This is how we do it here, this is why we do it, and these are the people bringing it to you!" Your practice should stand alone as a standard for all small businesses in your area to match. That's community leadership. That's impact on a scale that supersedes the smallness of back-pain ads on a bus-stop bench. This is "cultural authority," and you have to step into this with everything you've got.

Business is about people. It is about providing an incredible service to humanity, and it is about giving life to the people who run the systems. You cannot ignore the reality that the best businesses have the best people. The people on your team need to be intrinsically motivated, to be behaviorally matched to their positions, and to receive ongoing training and development.

In another revolutionary book of our time by Michael E. Gerber, *The Most Successful Small Business in the World,* he describes the Fifth Principle for creating the most successful small business:

A small business is a school in which its employees are students, with the intention, will, and determination to grow.

That sets the bar higher than anyone has ever placed it and gives us a perfect outline to follow. Read his book; it is a perfect companion to this work.

So if your staff members are the students, we need to make sure the teacher has the right students, the most effective curriculum, and the perfect environment for learning. The emotional tone of this environment is set by you, and you will need to keep the story of your practice in your head and on your lips every single day.

Before we talk more about your people, we have to make sure the teacher is awake. Now that you are on the fast track for sustainable growth, we need to look at two speed bumps that will force you to slow down and will throw your completion plan off course. As you might have guessed already, these two bumps exist in your head.

The first speed bump is having staff but not leveraging their talent. This severely restricts you from engaging in the other responsibilities you must meet as the owner of the practice. Too many doctors do the work that their chiropractic techs, with training, could and should do. You cannot achieve best practices on any scale by doing it all yourself. Stop laboring under the illusion that you need to control it all, and start experiencing the freedom of business and clinical teamwork.

The E-Myth term "technician" is a clear parallel to you, "the clinician." Your staff members are your practice's other technicians, so let them be technicians on a greater scale. They perform the tactical work of both the business systems and the appropriate clinical work.

Do you remember the sense of accomplishment and pride that you felt in school when you learned how to perform even the simplest aspects of patient exams? Remember the first time you used a sphygmomanometer or even pronounced it correctly? How about the first time you took an X-ray or used your "new eyes" to observe the posture of people in the mall, in restaurants, and thought to yourself, "Oh my, they could use my help." Well, how about spreading the love? Share that excitement and sense of significance that comes with being a competent technician with your people.

Chiropractic techs should be assisting you in the adjusting areas, helping with the initial consultation, and should be performing appropriate sections of the exam (as much as is legally permissible). They need to be trained so that they can take an active role in adjunctive care strategies that you order. Properly trained techs can reinforce the information you provide your patients by discussing activities of daily living, ergonomics, and self-care.

When the entire staff or "student body" gets pumped about seeing new patients, performing meaningful re-exams, and being in on the healing breakthroughs, your patients feel it, too. This is *practice building through people development*, and this creates marketing buzz. No one responds positively to hype anymore. Hype is what a copywriter or ad says about you. Buzz is what your people say. People like to be in a place that has *it* going on.

When you let your chiropractic techs engage at this level, everyone wins. The patients win because someone else is on their health-care team, the techs win because they have significance in your community, and you win because you are free to focus on the clinical activities that only a licensed chiropractor can do. Let go and experience the freedom.

Speed bump number two is being understaffed during peak hours, which results in missed re-exams, limited new patient access, and long wait times. You must hire in anticipation of growth. The chiropractor-as-employee wants to cut down overhead and will only hire when he or she is already too busy.

Entrepreneurs, though, know that they must prepare themselves and their business for growth, and that means hiring before they need the next person. When you have momentum, act! If you miss the window of growth, it closes and the practice eventually shrinks.

Another sign of scarcity behavior is not replacing an employee who left. This is a very common and costly mistake. The rest of the team is stretched to their mental and emotional capacities, and there is a breaking point. It is usually subtle at first, with a few missed appointments here and there, lack of new patients, and poor compliance. It takes, on average, six weeks to show up statistically, but once it does, it takes six months to get back on track. See what I mean?

Adequate Staffing for Quality and Growth

The E-Myth patient-centered chiropractic model has a personnel structure that is organized according to primary duties. The chiropractic techs then become personally responsible for the systems and procedures mandated by the following positions: front tech (responsible for coordinating the office visit), exam tech (responsible for assisting in the clinical care), and financial tech (responsible for the office financial policies). Each position is cross-trained yet accountable to its primary roles.

This patient-centered care model is dedicated to providing impeccable patient care regardless of the size of the practice. I recommend the following guidelines to assure quality service and to stimulate practice expansion.

A—One chiropractic tech is needed for a practice seeing up to 100 patient visits a week.

AA—Two chiropractic techs are needed for the practice seeing 101 to 250 patient visits a week.

AAA—Three chiropractic techs are needed for the practice seeing over 250 patient visits a week.

If your office performs attended therapies, then you may need to increase these numbers by one technician.

Recruiting the Best

Most chiropractors have no reliable hiring system for recruiting, training, and developing their staff. And so they end up keeping poor performers who make life miserable for the doctor and patients alike.

Let me tell you about Madison. Like most new employees, she was highly motivated yet needed some technical training. So she was motivated, but not competent. Madison was a fast learner, and her level of competency soon matched her level of enthusiasm for her position. Life was good for the doctor, fellow employees and, of course, the patients.

Yet as the practice grew, Madison had to interact with more patients and pick up her pace. You see, Madison preferred finishing one task completely before moving on to the next one. She liked people but preferred to do tasks like billing and data entry. When she was asked to perform a re-exam on a patient, she begrudgingly dragged herself away from the computer in a huff.

Over time, Madison continued to work hard, yet she suffered from "presenteeism." Her body was there; her mind and emotional commitment were somewhere else. She was still competent and did her work like a good employee should, but the thrill was gone. Soon after, she began making mistakes that she would never have committed before. Madison was now unmotivated and incompetent.

All of this is preventable. Sadly, most doctors adopt the attitude, "You just can't find good people anymore." There are two types of attitudes: useful and useless.

The useful attitude attracts solutions and cooperative people. We are more alike than different, and therefore, your people want the same things that you want. They are looking for a place that will challenge them with meaningful work, work that will call them to go beyond their self-imposed limitations. They want to be in a place that will teach them how to confront everyday problems and frustrations in a constructive way. They want an amiable, fair environment that recognizes and rewards them for their accomplishments.

Keep in mind that if your people's causal (personal) motivational needs are not being met, then the only way they can justify staying with you is to be motivated by incentive: "He promised me a bonus and a raise." Or fear: "If I continue to do whatever it is I'm doing, at least I won't be fired."

By causal motivation I mean that each staff member has his or her personal cause, his or her personal interests, attitudes, and values that need to be met through the work that the staff member does. When the job satisfies their personal motivational needs, they choose to be enrolled in the vision and mission.

Hiring Is a System, Not a Feeling

Have you ever hired someone who couldn't work with your team? Typically, people are hired for their skills and fired for their attitude.

Did you know that most people hired in the interview process are hired by the heart, not the head? The decision is often emotional because you need someone yesterday.

According to a Michigan State University study, "14 percent of hiring decisions based on the interview process alone are correct." In this competitive hiring market, people are trained in résumé writing and taught how to interview. Too often the person you interviewed never shows up on the job. You need more reliable tools. You need a benchmark and a hiring system.

A benchmark is something that serves as a standard or point of reference by which others may be measured. Now that you have the attitudinal benchmark that Michael gave us, the one that says employees must possess the intention, will, and determination to grow, all you need do is administer the appropriate assessments to see if your potential hire matches that benchmark.

The benchmarking system asks the question, "If the position could speak, what would it say?" We know that certain behavioral needs will never be met in a chiropractic practice, and the same is true for the motivators or values. Therefore, the staff may give lip service to your story and vision, but never be enrolled. A benchmark system assists you in finding, retaining, and developing the right talent in your office. School is in session! For more information on benchmarking, go to www.michaelegerber.com/co-author.

High Touch

We have been focusing heavily on systems and for good reason. We want you to be free of the routine and simple processes so that your business embodies the principled human qualities of the people in your practice. Your business has to attract good people and make them great. This is why Michael describes your business as a school. Only the best and motivated need apply. Only the best and motivated get a role in the story of your practice. Do you see why this is so important? Can you imagine a place like that? I hope so, because that is what you are going to create.

The students and the teacher need to connect with the "why" before you teach them the "how." I want you and your staff to get your "why" on! Why do you adjust a spine? Why do you perform examinations? Why is it important to have financial systems? Why do you teach healthy lifestyle choices? Why do the systems matter? Get the first things right and the rest is easy.

In Dov Seidman's book, *How: Why How We Do Anything Means Everything . . . in Business (and in Life)*, he states, "The tapestry of human behavior is so diverse, so rich, and so global that it represents a rare opportunity, the opportunity to outbehave the competition."

You and your people need ongoing soft skill training if your practice is going to "outbehave" the competition. It's not what you say as much as it is how you say it. It's not the procedure; it's how you do it.

Let's make a distinction between hard skills and soft skills. Hard skills are those you learned in chiropractic college, and the procedural and tactical training your staff received. While hard skills are important, focusing only on the technical competencies leaves most of us naked in the real world.

Soft skills are people skills. They are a fusion of emotional intelligence (EI) and nonverbal intelligence (NVI). Soft skills close the gap between what science knows about human needs and what most businesses do to meet them.

Emotional intelligence is the awareness that our emotions, positive and negative, affect other people. It is the ability to regulate and adapt our behavior so that our interaction with others is a positive experience.

Nonverbal intelligence is the awareness that we communicate our internal states through our body language, facial expressions, and tone of voice. And yes, even the way we dress. It is the ability to accentuate our positive feelings and respect toward others by taking charge of these nonverbal signals.

Practices that create healthy relationships thrive. Chiropractic care is relationship building. We open the relationship during the new patient interview, define it in our report of findings, and develop it on each and every office visit or phone conversation.

I like to look at a relationship as two circles coming together. You are responsible for your circle, your half of the relationship. So your higher standard of excellence is authenticity through soft skills. We have set a new standard for your practice. Now let's see what Michael has to say about associates. ❖

On the Subject
of Associates

Michael E. Gerber

Associate yourself with men of good quality if you esteem your own
reputation, for 'tis better to be alone than in bad company.

—George Washington

If you're a sole practitioner—that is, you're selling only yourself—then your chiropractic company called a practice will
never make the leap to a chiropractic company called a business.
The progression from practice to business to enterprise demands
that you hire other chiropractors to do what you do (or don't do).
Contractors call these people subcontractors; for our purposes, we'll
refer to them as associate chiropractors.

Contractors know that subs can be a huge problem. It's no less
true for chiropractors. Until you face this special business problem,
your practice will never become a business, and your business will
certainly never become an enterprise.

Long ago, God said, "Let there be chiropractors. And
so they never forget who they are in my creation, let them be

damned forever to hire people exactly like themselves." Enter the associates.

Merriam-Webster's Collegiate Dictionary, Eleventh Edition, defines *sub* as "under, below, secretly; inferior to." If associate chiropractors are like sub-chiropractors, you could define an associate as "an inferior individual contracted to perform part or all of another's contract."

In other words, you, the chiropractor, make a conscious decision to hire someone "inferior" to you to fulfill *your* commitment to *your* patient, for which you are ultimately and solely liable.

Why in the world do we do these things to ourselves? Where will this madness lead? It seems the blind are leading the blind, and the blind are paying others to do it. And when a chiropractor is blind, you *know* there's a problem!

It's time to step out of the darkness and come into the light. Forget about being Mr. Nice Guy—it's time to do things that work.

Solving the Associate Chiropractor Problem

Let's say you're about to hire an associate chiropractor. Someone who has specific skills: technique, rehab, whatever. It all starts with choosing the right personnel. After all, these are people to whom you are delegating your responsibility and for whose behavior you are completely liable. Do you really want to leave that choice to chance? Are you that much of a gambler? I doubt it.

If you've never worked with your new associate, how do you really know he or she is skilled? For that matter, what does "skilled" mean?

For you to make an intelligent decision about this associate chiropractor, you must have a working definition of the word *skilled*. Your challenge is to know *exactly* what your expectations are, then to make sure your other chiropractors operate with precisely the same expectations. Failure here almost assures a breakdown in your relationship.

I want you to write the following on a piece of paper: "By *skilled*, I mean . . . " Once you create your personal definition, it will become a standard for you and your practice, for your patients, and for your associate chiropractors.

A standard, according to *Webster's Eleventh*, is something "set up and established by authority as a rule for the measure of quantity, weight, extent, value, or quality."

Thus, your goal is to establish a measure of quality control, a standard of skill, which you will apply to all your associate chiropractors. More important, you are also setting a standard for the performance of your company.

By creating standards for your selection of other chiropractors— standards of skill, performance, integrity, financial stability, and experience—you have begun the powerful process of building a practice that can operate exactly as you expect it to.

By carefully thinking about exactly what to expect, you have already begun to improve your practice.

In this enlightened state, you will see the selection of your associates as an opportunity to define what you (1) intend to provide for your patients, (2) expect from your employees, and (3) demand for your life.

Powerful stuff, isn't it? Are you up to it? Are you ready to feel your rising power?

Don't rest on your laurels just yet. Defining those standards is only the first step you need to take. The second step is to create an *associate chiropractor development system.*

An associate chiropractor development system is an action plan designed to tell you what you are looking for in an associate. It includes the exact benchmarks, accountabilities, timing of fulfillment, and budget you will assign to the process of looking for associate chiropractors, identifying them, recruiting them, interviewing them, training them, managing their work, auditing their performance, compensating them, reviewing them regularly, and terminating or rewarding them for their performance.

All of these things must be documented—actually *written down*—if they're going to make any difference to you, your associate chiropractors, your managers, or your bank account!

And then you've got to persist with that system, come hell or high water. Just as Ray Kroc did. Just as Walt Disney did. Just as Sam Walton did.

This leads us to our next topic of discussion: the subject of *estimating*. But first, let's listen to what Dr. Frank has to say on the subject of associate chiropractors. ✤

CHAPTER

12

Most Associateships Don't Work and What to Do About It

Dr. Frank Sovinsky

To everything there is a season, and a time to every purpose under heaven.
—Ecclesiastes 3:1

Michael is absolutely right. If you are to follow the path of the entrepreneur to its logical destiny—the enterprise—then an associate is in your future. Now what you have to get is this: This entrepreneurial path has milestones to exceed before you realize your destiny, and there are no shortcuts. There are many reasons doctors make the decision to hire an associate. Yet only one is logical. You hire an associate only when your practice is a mature business. If you hire an associate in the infancy or adolescent stages of practice, you will stunt its growth and doom it to mediocrity. Premature hiring and faulty planning strains the systems, drains the flow of both money and resources, and adds additional managerial drama to your already-overworked life.

A mature practice has met most of the benchmarks set forth in the business plan. It can afford to pay an associate. Let's get clear about this. When I say afford another doctor, I mean that many of your personal financial goals have been met. You have eliminated debt and have some passive income streaming in from other solid, reliable investments. This is not an idealistic standard. It is a utilitarian reality of best practices.

The practice battlefield is littered with the casualties of associateships gone bad. The walking wounded of the "associateship experiment" comes from both sides of the engagement, the host doctor and the associate. Most associateship-driven practices do not work. The traditional associateship model needs to be dismantled as we move toward a more socially responsible Chiropractic Associate Development Program.

We rarely talk about this problem, and when we do, it is to whine and complain. The host doctor complains, "These young doctors don't know what it is like to work hard. When I started this practice I worked sixty hours a week." And the associate doctors whine, "I can't believe he makes all of that money as a result of my hard work and only pays me this small percentage."

The traditional model is flawed, and it produces two types of associates, the winner and the whiner. The winner is a highly talented and skilled doctor who soon wakes up to the stark limitations of his current situation and will sever the arrangement within six to eighteen months.

The whiner feels emotionally entitled, lacks confidence, has poor interpersonal skills, and is unwilling to pull his own weight and produce. He will never leave!

The Seven Deadly Reasons for Hiring an Associate

My company, DC Mentors, has gained valuable insight through mentoring the walking wounded from the "associateship experiment." There is a predictable irrationality that moves most doctors into premature associateships. Let's open this discussion with the seven deadly reasons for hiring an associate along with a few salient comments.

Reason 1: "I need someone to cover my practice so that I can go on vacation."

This is a sign the doctor is working *in* the practice and has not worked enough *on* the practice. We all need rejuvenation days to stay focused and to enjoy time with family. If you plan your breaks and have what I call a "rejuvenation system," all you need to do is refer to a trusted colleague in your absence.

Reason 2: "I need someone to help me adjust during the peak times because we are too busy."

While this situation can occur, we've found it is definitely the exception rather than the rule. With efficient, effective procedures and staff training, most DCs can handle the volume of a thriving practice without adding another chiropractor.

Reason 3: "I need someone who will help me build the practice."

The practice needs to be mature and self-sustaining before you want to grow it to the next level. Your reputation as a business should already be providing you with a steady stream of referrals. Marketing and public relations is expertise few associates have.

Reason 4: "I need someone of like mind to make it more fun and put some life back into the practice."

A community of like minds is nurturing. Yet there are many strategies that are more cost-effective without the hassles of "buying a friend."

Reason 5: "I need a break. I want someone who will help me manage the practice and give me more free time to do other things."

This is another symptom of abdicating the role of manager. An associate rarely meets the criteria we outlined in chapters 7 and 8 for the position of manager.

Reason 6: "I need someone qualified to perform my exams."

A certified and skilled chiropractic technician can, in most cases, perform exams to the standards you require.

Reason 7: "I need to hire my relative (daughter, son, wife, husband, son-in -law, daughter-in-law) who is about to graduate."

Or "The patient I referred to chiropractic college is about ready to graduate and I promised them a job."

This is a big one. Good chiropractors can make poor decisions because of their emotional biases. It keeps them from reaching the affluent "equity goal line."

When the host doctor hires a family member or friend, it represents nepotism at its best and at its worse. It can have disastrous results.

The hazard that we see is this: a family member, friend, or former patient usually comes with a very well-entrenched level of entitlement. Because of the family bond, the associate doctor may feel a false sense of security and the work ethic can become compromised. Another problem can surface if the host doctor's practice has a flawed business model or poorly defined systems. In this case, what started as a legacy is passed on as a generational malignancy.

When the Time Is Right

Once you have your practice moving and growing in all the right places, you will need to—once again—innovate, quantify, and orchestrate the next important system, the Chiropractic Associate Development Program.

This system begins with recruiting and hiring the right candidates. Remember this important distinction: An associate is an employee of the business, and since a business is a school, the associate is a student. This employee is responsible for the tactical work directly related to the Clinical Department and may, on occasion, contribute some strategic work for you.

The Chiropractic Associate Development Program is created for two types of candidates, the chiropractic "intern" and the "clinically seasoned" chiropractor.

The chiropractic intern is typically a recent graduate who is highly motivated, yet not clinically seasoned. This candidate will need more in-depth training to include clinical case management, along with all the other processes and system training that fellow employees learn in your school.

The clinically seasoned chiropractic associate will need to learn your chiropractic technique, treatment protocols, and case management as well. These associates' learning curves may be faster, yet they may resist adopting your ideas because they are used to doing it "their way."

There is only "One way we do it here," and that must be documented and adhered to. The clinically seasoned associate is most often a bright, caring, and talented doctor who prefers to be a clinician (technician) and is not motivated or interested in developing his or her entrepreneurial capacities.

The life span of the associate relationship can range from eighteen months all the way to your equity goal line. You might discover that rotating your interns every eighteen to twenty-four months works best for you and your business plan.

The success or failure of this more socially responsible model rests on your skill set as a mentor. Success follows right intent and right actions. As a mentor, your role is to bring out the best in all employees and help them eliminate habits of mediocrity and complacency. This can be one of the most rewarding relationships you ever develop.

There is one other plan for succession. The DC Mentors "Successorship Practice" has met all of the business plan benchmarks. The recruiting process and plan for succession is fast-tracked as the doctor is ready to pass the baton to a qualified successor, not just sell the practice equity. The recruiting process is more stringent, as this candidate must be an "intrapreneur" with a flair for business development, and a passion to do it within your practice. To learn more, go to www.michaelegerber.com/co-author.

We recognize that bringing another doctor into the practice can be a win-win scenario and has a place in the careers of many doctors. However, timing is everything. Now that we have shed some light on a misunderstood practice, let's add the next piece of the E-Myth puzzle and see what Michael has to say about estimating your fees. ❖

CHAPTER 13

On the Subject of Estimating

Michael E. Gerber

The way a Chihuahua goes about eating a dead elephant is to take a bite and be very present with that bite. In spiritual growth, the definitive act is to take one step and let tomorrow's step take care of itself.
—William H. Houff, *Infinity in Your Hand: A Guide for the Spiritually Curious*

One of the greatest weaknesses of chiropractors is accurately estimating how long appointments will take and then scheduling their patients accordingly. *Webster's Eleventh* defines estimate as "a rough or approximate calculation." Anyone who has visited a chiropractor's waiting room knows that those estimates can be rough indeed.

Do you want to see someone who gives you a rough approximation? What if your chiropractor gave you a rough approximation of your condition?

The fact is that we can predict many things we don't typically predict. For example, there are ways to learn the truth about people who come in complaining about neck or lower-back pain. Look at the steps of the process. Most of the things you do are standard, so develop a step-by-step system and stick to it.

In my book *The E-Myth Manager*, I raised eyebrows by suggesting that medical doctors eliminate the waiting room. Why? You don't need it if you're always on time. The same goes for a chiropractic practice. If you're always on time, then your patients don't have to wait.

What if a chiropractor made this promise: on time, every time, as promised, or we pay for it.

"Impossible!" chiropractors cry. "Each patient is different. We simply can't know how long each appointment will take."

Do you follow this? Since chiropractors believe they're incapable of knowing how to organize their time, they build a practice based on lack of knowing and lack of control. They build a practice based on estimates.

I once had a chiropractor ask me, "What happens when someone comes in for a routine adjustment and we discover they were in an auto accident since their last visit? How can we deal with someone so unexpected? How can we give proper care and stay on schedule?" My first thought was that it's not being dealt with now. Few chiropractors are able to give generously of their time. Ask anyone who's been to a chiropractor's office lately. It's chaos.

The solution is interest, attention, analysis. Try detailing what you do at the beginning of an interaction, what you do in the middle, and what you do at the end. How long does each take? In the absence of such detailed, quantified standards, everything ends up being an estimate, and a poor estimate at that.

However, a practice organized around a system, with adequate staff to run it, has time for proper attention. It's built right into the system.

Too many chiropractors have grown accustomed to thinking in terms of estimates without thinking about what the term really means. Is it any wonder many chiropractic practices are in trouble?

Enlightened chiropractors, in contrast, banish the word *estimate* from their vocabulary. When it comes to estimating, just say no!

"But you can never be exact," chiropractors have told me for years. "Close, maybe. But never exact."

I have a simple answer to that: *You have to be.* You simply can't afford to be inexact. You can't accept inexactness in yourself or in your chiropractic practice.

You can't go to work every day believing that your practice, the work you do, and the commitments you make are all too complex and unpredictable to be exact. With a mindset like that, you're doomed to run a sloppy ship. A ship that will eventually sink and suck you down with it.

This is so easy to avoid. Sloppiness—in both thought and action—is the root cause of your frustrations.

The solution to those frustrations is clarity. Clarity gives you the ability to set a clear direction, which fuels the momentum you need to grow your business.

Clarity, direction, momentum—they all come from insisting on exactness.

But how do you create exactness in a hopelessly inexact world? The answer is this. You discover the exactness in your practice by refusing to do any work that can't be controlled exactly.

The only other option is to analyze the market, determine where the opportunities are, and then organize your practice to be the exact provider of the services you've chosen to offer.

Two choices, and only two choices: (1) evaluate your practice and then limit yourself to the tasks you know you can do exactly, or (2) start all over by analyzing the market, identifying the key opportunities in that market, and building a practice that operates exactly.

What you cannot do, what you must refuse to do, from this day forward, is to allow yourself to operate with an inexact mindset. It will lead you to ruin.

Which leads us inexorably back to the word I have been using through this book: *systems.*

Who makes estimates? Only chiropractors who are unclear about exactly how to do the task in question. Only chiropractors whose experience has taught them that if something can go wrong, it will—and to them!

I'm not suggesting that a *systems solution* will guarantee that you always perform exactly as promised. But I am saying that a systems solution will faithfully alert you when you're going off track, and will do it before you have to pay the price for it.

In short, with a systems solution in place, your need to estimate will be a thing of the past, both because you have organized your practice to anticipate mistakes, and because you have put into place the system to do something about those mistakes before they blow up.

There's this, too: To make a promise you intend to keep places a burden on you and your managers to dig deeply into how you intend to keep it. Such a burden will transform your intentions and increase your attention to detail.

With the promise will come dedication. With dedication will come integrity. With integrity will come consistency. With consistency will come results you can count on. And results you can count on mean that you get exactly what you hoped for at the outset of your practice: the true pride of ownership that every chiropractor should experience.

This brings us to the subject of *patients*. Who are they? Why do they come to you? How can you identify yours? And who *should* your patients be? But first, let's listen to what Dr. Frank has to say about estimating. ✤

CHAPTER 14

The Best Things in Life Are Fees

Dr. Frank Sovinsky

Price is what you pay. Value is what you get.

—Warren Buffett

Fees are the best things in life when they are affordable to your patients and profitable for you. That's the message. Make your care affordable by creating equitable financial policies. Make it profitable through systematization and a more efficient office design. When you do this, your practice will be financially hassle-free, and it will outperform the competition. I guarantee it.

Fees are the best things in life when you no longer think about them. Imagine never worrying about whether or not patients have insurance that covers chiropractic or trying to fight for dollars if they do. Imagine the patients' relief when they no longer have to worry about their bill getting declined by their insurance company.

Imagine being free of the mindless habit of writing off a patient's bill because you never expected to be paid the full amount anyway! Imagine the relief patients feel when they know the charges in your office will not use up all their benefits, the benefits they would like to have in reserve just in case they need other health care.

Imagine what it would be like to hear a patient say he or she can't afford your care and have it not affect you because you know it is a fair exchange. You own it.

That's what I mean about fees being the best thing in your practice. Fees that work for you and your patients foster healthy relationships and promote patient accountability. You are reading this book, so I think it's safe to assume that you don't think I am talking about national health care as the solution to the fee dilemma.

To my colleagues outside the United States, I know most of you do not enjoy anything resembling insurance equality. Many of you have had government care come and go. In talking with you, I know you don't share this obsession that your American colleagues have with high fees, upcoding, and the like. So you have one less thing to unlearn; yet you will still have to set the right fee.

Our profession has a history that has influenced our culture concerning money and patient care. As you know, we fought for and continue to protect the right to take care of patients. Our predecessors agreed that patients should have access to our care, and that if they have insurance, then their insurance company should not discriminate and limit patient choice. So we fought for the patient; yet somewhere in the fight, many doctors got off track.

By default, too many chiropractors were seduced by the good times and high reimbursement. The feeding frenzy caused some to slip into the abyss of entitlement along with their patients. An entire industry led by billing software, collection agencies, family plan schemes, yearly contracts, and insurance upcoding seminars has swooped in to make sure you get what's coming to you. But it may not be what you want.

If we pull back the covers, it's very simple. You have a service that you are certain will transform the lives of those who use it. That service has value to you as the provider, and to the patient, who is the receiver. There are principles and laws that govern fair exchange, and this topic is much too deep to cover in this chapter.

Yet we trust that chapters 3 and 4 got you thinking more clearly and interested to learn more about the topic of money.

There are no secrets about money, just common sense and integrity. That's why you are reading this book. You have both.

This is a book about truth and ethical business practices—the E-Myth ideals applied to the business of chiropractic. I want to draw more wisdom from Michael's book *The Most Successful Small Business in the World* for our discussion. In this work, he reveals the Fourth Principle:

"A small business must be sustainable through all economic conditions, in all markets, providing meaningful, highly differentiated results to all of its customers."

Read that Fourth Principle as often as it takes to hear the message between the lines. When you follow principles, most of your decisions are made for you. So what does this principle have to do with our topic, fees? Everything.

Your fee must be profitable enough to sustain you regardless of economic recessions or market conditions. As the owner of your business, the entrepreneur, you have several ways to do business in your community: entrepreneur to enterprise, entrepreneur to government, or entrepreneur to the individual consumer.

The entrepreneur to enterprise is doing business with an insurance company, HMO, or PPO, and is dependent on the policies and rules of the enterprise. You are not in control unless you decide to remove yourself from their system. Policies and reimbursement schedules are dictated by the carrier. You either accept the rules or get kicked to the curb.

The entrepreneur to government arrangement is usually mandated with fixed fees and treatment guidelines. In the United States, it's Medicare. In Canada, there remain a few provinces that have similar programs, and a few other countries worldwide are moving in this direction. You have little if any choice as to whether or not you participate. Don't mess with the government.

My biggest problem with insurance as it is, or government programs as they may become, is this: Most of the time, the policies limit the patients' possibilities. Nothing should get in the way of the patients' health-care needs and their choice of doctor.

The entrepreneur to the individual consumer of your service, the patient, is where you can wield your greatest influence. Your chances for building an economy-proof practice is in this business model.

What to Charge

So fees are the best thing in your future, and you need to get them right. You have to determine who your target market is and make your fee reasonable for that market.

What is the right fee? Look at the demographics of your community. More affluent patients are willing and able to pay a slightly higher fee, yet value and the terms "customary" and "reasonable" still apply. Do not survey other offices because you may be replicating failure. Remember, you are going to set the mark for best business practices in your community.

The right fee is the one where you can look the patient in the eye and without hesitation say, "This is what I charge." The right fee is the one that you would pay without reservation. Would you be able to pay for care in your office?

Do not value the price of the adjustment based upon the results you get. Some adjustments are life-altering, yet they are not priceless. And do not set your fees according to all of your special training and extra procedures you perform. The reality is that patients do not and, in the foreseeable future, will not see you as a medical specialist.

Getting Overhead under Your Feet

Now on to the subject of overhead and profitability. You have to get your overhead under your feet. The "bigger is better" model is burying too many doctors in an avalanche of stress and forcing them to charge higher fees.

Be careful of the 4,000-square-foot mega-office. In most cases, doctors get too busy, and they decide that the only solution is to get a bigger office and add staff. Believe it or not, most never consider that the solution is to get better systems and improved office design. For example, do you have enough adjusting tables? Do you have the appropriate number of exam rooms? Do you have a room designated specifically for reports to patients? Are all of these things placed in the most efficient place they can be? Or is there a big private office in the middle of everything taking up valuable space? Sometimes a renovation and redesign is a better way to go.

Solving the right problem and working on the business can cause benchmarks to be exceeded, and in some cases, a bigger space and additional technicians is the right decision. This is usually the exception, though, not the rule. The "bigger is better" business model will not work in the coming years. As a matter of fact, it really isn't working now.

You are obligated as the owner of your business to trim the fat of your practice without compromising patient care or limiting reinvesting in your business for growth. When you make that decision and you make that happen, the fees you charge will be affordable and you will be profitable. Now let's see what revelations Michael has in store for us as he discusses the subject of patients. ✤

CHAPTER 15

On the Subject of Patients

Michael E. Gerber

Some patients I see are actually draining into their bodies the diseased thoughts of their minds.

> —Zachary T. Bercovitz, *Wisdom for the Soul:*
> *Five Millennia of Prescriptions for Spiritual Healing*

W hen it comes to the practice of chiropractic, the best definition of patients I've ever heard is this:

Patients: *very special people who drive most chiropractors crazy.*

Does that work for you?

After all, it's a rare patient who shows any appreciation for what a chiropractor has to go through to do the job as promised. Don't they always think the price is too high? And don't they focus on problems, broken promises, and the mistakes they think you make, rather than all the ways you bend over backward to give them what they need?

Do you ever hear other chiropractors voice these complaints? More to the point, have you ever voiced them yourself? Well, you're not alone. I have yet to meet a chiropractor who doesn't suffer from a strong case of patient confusion.

Patient confusion is about:

- what your patient really wants;
- how to communicate effectively with your patient;
- how to keep your patient happy;
- how to deal with patient dissatisfaction; and
- whom to call a patient.

Confusion 1: What Your Patient Really Wants

Your patients aren't just people; they're very specific kinds of people. Let me share with you the six categories of patients as seen from the E-Myth marketing perspective: (1) tactile patients, (2) neutral patients, (3) withdrawal patients, (4) experimental patients, (5) transitional patients, and (6) traditional patients.

Your entire marketing strategy must be based on which type of patient you are dealing with. Each of the six patient types spends money on chiropractic services for very different, and identifiable, reasons. These are:

- Tactile patients get their major gratification from interacting with other people.
- Neutral patients get their major gratification from interacting with inanimate objects (computers, cars, information).
- Withdrawal patients get their major gratification from interacting with ideas (thoughts, concepts, stories).
- Experimental patients rationalize their buying decisions by perceiving that what they bought is new, revolutionary, and innovative.
- Transitional patients rationalize their buying decisions by perceiving that what they bought is dependable and reliable.

- Traditional patients rationalize their buying decisions by perceiving that what they bought is cost-effective, a good deal, and worth the money.

In short:
- If your patient is tactile, you have to emphasize the *people* of your practice.
- If your patient is neutral, you have to emphasize the *technology* of your practice.
- If your patient is a withdrawal patient, you have to emphasize the *idea* of your practice.
- If your patient is experimental, you have to emphasize the *uniqueness* of your practice.
- If your patient is transitional, you have to emphasize the *dependability* of your practice.
- If your patient is traditional, you have to talk about the *financial competitiveness* of your practice.

What your patients want is determined by who they are. Who they are is regularly demonstrated by what they do. Think about the patients with whom you do business. Ask yourself: In which of the categories would I place them? What do they do for a living?

If your patient is a mechanical engineer, for example, it's probably safe to assume he's a neutral patient. If another one of your patients is a cardiologist, she's probably tactile. Accountants tend to be traditional, and software engineers are often experimental.

Having an idea about which categories your patients may fall into is very helpful to figuring out what they want. Of course, there's no exact science to it, and human beings constantly defy stereotypes. So don't take my word for it. You'll want to make your own analysis of the patients you serve.

Confusion 2: How to Communicate Effectively with Your Patient

The next step in the patient satisfaction process is to decide how to magnify the characteristics of your practice that are most likely to appeal to your preferred category of patient. That begins with what marketing people call your *positioning strategy*.

What do I mean by *positioning* your practice? You position your practice with words. A few well-chosen words to tell your patients exactly what they want to hear. In marketing lingo, those words are called your USP, or unique selling proposition.

For example, if you are targeting tactile patients (ones who love people), your USP could be: "Wellness Care, where the feelings of people *really* count!"

If you are targeting experimental patients (ones who love new, revolutionary things), your USP could be: "Wellness Care, where living on the edge is a way of life!" In other words, when they choose to schedule an appointment with you, they can count on both your services and equipment to be on the cutting edge of the chiropractic industry.

Is this starting to make sense? Do you see how the ordinary things most chiropractors do to get patients can be done in a significantly more effective way?

Once you understand the essential principles of marketing the E-Myth way, the strategies by which you attract patients can make an enormous difference in your market share.

Confusion 3: How to Keep Your Patient Happy

Let's say you've overcome the first two confusions. Great. Now how do you keep your patient happy?

Very simple . . . just keep your promise! And make sure your patient *knows* you kept your promise every step of the way.

In short, giving your patients what they think they want is the key to keeping your patients (or anyone else, for that matter) really happy.

If your patients need to interact with people (high touch, tactile), make certain that they do.

If they need to interact with things (high-tech, neutral), make certain that they do.

If they need to interact with ideas (in their head, withdrawal), make certain that they do.

And so forth.

At E-Myth, we call this your *patient fulfillment system*. It's the step-by-step process by which you do the task you've contracted to do and deliver what you've promised—on time, every time.

But what happens when your patients are *not* happy? What happens when you've done everything I've mentioned here and your patient is still dissatisfied?

Confusion 4: How to Deal with Patient Dissatisfaction

If you have followed each step up to this point, patient dissatisfaction will be rare. But it can and will still occur—people are people, and some people will always find a way to be dissatisfied with something. Here's what to do about it:

- Always listen to what your patients are saying. And never interrupt while they're saying it.
- After you're sure you've heard all of your patient's complaint, make absolutely certain you understand what she said by phrasing a question, such as: "Can I repeat what you've just told me, Ms. Harton, to make absolutely certain I understand you?"
- Secure your patient's acknowledgment that you have heard her complaint accurately.
- Apologize for whatever your patient thinks you did that dissatisfied her, even if you didn't do it!
- After your patient has acknowledged your apology, ask her exactly what would make her happy.
- Repeat what your patient told you would make her happy, and get her acknowledgment that you have heard correctly.
- If at all possible, give your patient exactly what she has asked for.

You may be thinking, "But what if my patient wants something totally impossible?" Don't worry. If you've followed my recommendations to the letter, what your patient asks for will seldom seem unreasonable.

Confusion 5: Whom to Call a Patient

At this stage, it's important to ask yourself some questions about the kind of patients you hope to attract to your practice:

- Which types of patients would you most like to do business with?
- Where do you see your real market opportunities?
- Who would you like to work with, provide services to, and position your business for?

In short, *it's all up to you*. No mystery. No magic. Just a systematic process for shaping your practice's future. But you must have the passion to pursue the process. And you must be absolutely clear about every aspect of it.

Until you know your patients as well as you know yourself.

Until all your complaints about patients are a thing of the past.

Until you accept the undeniable fact that patient acquisition and patient satisfaction are more science than art.

But unless you're willing to grow your practice, you'd better not follow any of these recommendations. Because if you do what I'm suggesting, it's going to grow.

This brings us to the subject of *growth*. But first, let's listen to what Dr. Frank has to say about patients. ❖

CHAPTER 16

See the Person in the Patient

Dr. Frank Sovinsky

Treat people as if they were what they ought to be and you will help them become what they are capable of becoming.

—Johann Wolfgang Von Goethe

W hen I tell my audiences, "Practice would be so much easier if it weren't for the patients," they usually laugh. It seems that the "us against them" mentality is more readily exposed if we can keep it light. The relationships we develop with our patients can be rewarding and frustrating at the same time.

So why do we get so frustrated when patients reject our offers to help or if they quit before something wonderful is about to happen? Maybe it's just that certain kinds of patients frustrate us. Is that why we label them as being a good or bad patient?

We might spin that first statement and say, "Practice would be so much easier if the right kind of patients would come in (good patients)." I have even heard doctors take that attitude to a much more doctor-centric viewpoint and proclaim, "If a patient knew what I knew, they would do what I do."

Let me tell you about my patient, Peter. He was a tall, slightly built businessman. He was demanding, cold, and not happy to be in my office. He wanted his feet fixed—now! I rubbed them, I taped them, and I fit him for orthotics. I jammed blocks under him, used an activator, stretched him, and forced microcurrents through his body. I gave him nutritional advice and even attempted stress counseling. I did everything but put leeches on him.

Peter never followed my treatment schedule, and when he did show up he was late! Then he demanded more time and attention at my busiest hour, always backing up my schedule. He complained about my fees, so I cut him and his family a deal. Then, as they say, he was lost to follow-up.

I did not know then what I know now, and I am eager to have this next conversation with you. Can I share my thoughts on patient-centered care? Can I show you a way to enjoy each and every person that walks through your door?

Did you know that people are more alike than they are different? Yet these differences can lead to confusion and missed opportunities for cooperation toward a common goal. We want to help, and they want that help. As I see it, the doctor-patient relationship is opened during the consultation and exam, defined when we relate our findings, and then developed each and every visit. This is a process with a human quality, a system with a higher purpose and softer touch.

Most chiropractors are out of touch with the real world. They often live in the idealistic cocoon of their college experience or try to reproduce the motivational attributes of their last seminar experience. In E-Myth terms this leads to product-centered—not patient-centered—service.

Doctor-centered interactions focus on what the doctor needs to say about the product, chiropractic care. In sharp contrast, patient-centered interactions focus on what the patient needs to hear; it "relates" to them.

It's obvious that you have decided to break from the pack, and your first shift in perspective is to see the person in the patient. Something alarming happens when a new person walks into your office. Suddenly this person becomes a "patient." A preconceived relationship is already in place in both of your heads. You're the doctor and he or she is the patient, and you must treat the person as such, whatever that is.

Behind the label of patient is a person. This person is not a new patient, established patient, or good or bad patient, and he or she certainly is not a statistic. Patients don't care to know everything you know. They want you to care for them as they are. It's not just neck pain, it's *their* neck pain.

It's Not What You Are Saying, It's How You Are Saying It

Each of us has experienced this frustrating scenario. Everything seems to be going great. The patient appears to be committed to the care plan and happy with the results. Then the patient starts missing appointments and eventually drops out of sight. What's going on? Is he out of money and time? Did she leave because she feels better or feels no change? Or did the patient just lose interest because you lost interest?

Sometimes our "psychological immune system" is overactive as it kicks in to helps us avoid the pain of rejection. So we make up a story to preserve our image and to stay positive. We tell ourselves that the patients who left the practice just don't care enough about their health and that they just didn't get it.

Yet the number one reason patients leave your practice is this: They feel neglected, not respected, not taken seriously, and not heard. They perceive your indifference.

Patients are more attuned neurologically to respond to your feelings than to your words. The truth is patients may never openly disclose their frustration or disappointment with you, your care, or your staff. So they cancel appointments, saying they feel better or they feel worse. Or the one you can't get enough of, "I don't have the time or the money right now." Thanks, but no thanks. They're just not that into you.

While it is popular to use the buzz phrase "patient-centered care," few people appreciate that this means all patients, not just the ones who agree with us and show their appreciation.

Until now, doctors have assumed that patient noncompliance was a lack of education. We are not the only profession with this challenge, yet because of the size of our market, we feel its effect much more profoundly, and we can no longer ignore the cause.

Certainly patients need to be informed about their spinal health and the consequences of going through life with misalignments, subluxations, or neuroarticular dysfunctions. I am not being politically correct, I just don't want you to get hung up on a word and miss the point of this chapter.

I think we can agree that patients need contextual information and guidance concerning other strategies and lifestyle choices that will contribute to their well-being. I do agree that we are "hands on" teachers.

Yet the most effective teachers you and I have had were effective communicators. They knew their audience. They understood psychographics. They made certain that you received the message. You will need to become a skilled communicator. Skilled communicators

- initiate and develop business relationships in positive ways;
- successfully interact with a wide range of people;
- adapt their behavior for enhanced communication;
- communicate with others in ways that are clear, considerate and understandable; and
- treat others fairly, regardless of personal biases or beliefs.

Psychographics Are the "Core Muscles" of Marketing

In chapter 5, Michael introduced this concept and he expanded on this topic in the last chapter when he talked about the six patient types. We both agree that psychographics and its ethical application sit at the core of your new patient attraction, patient compliance, and patient fulfillment systems.

We are going to bridge the gap between what science knows about what humans need and what doctors and their techs do.

Psychographics are the psychological characteristics of our patient population, a graph of their psyche. This includes their mental frames concerning health and healing, their individual communication needs, and their expectations of you as their health-care provider.

My company, DC Mentors, has innovated, quantified, and orchestrated patient-centered procedures in hundreds of practices worldwide. These procedures were created from emerging scholarship in the disciplines of psychology, sociology, and neuroscience and tested in a host of socioeconomic environments. I want to share a few of the key psychographic principles with you. I want to inspire you to become a skillful communicator.

Mental Frames

People want to feel good. And feeling good makes them happy. In a very real sense we are in the feel-good business. Patients want to feel better than they did when they walked into your office. Less pain and diminished suffering are only part of that. They want to be affirmed and validated. They come to your office because you care, you listen, and you and your team are interested in them, and are interesting people to be around.

The startling reality is this: The vast majority of people in your potential target market view the chiropractic adjustments as an elective procedure. This is definitely true for most insurance programs, and this trend is likely to continue for the next decade.

Other elective procedures include Botox injections, Lasik eye surgery, cosmetic dentistry, massage, and acupuncture, to name a few. For some people, the out-of-pocket expense of elective procedures is a luxury that they are not willing to pay for unless the value is compelling to them.

Let me share a few other psychographic pearls with you:

- Patients come for the right reason, theirs. Their pain, condition, or circumstance is limiting them in some capacity. This limitation is the real problem, and they want you to help them solve it.

- Patients seek your help because what they are doing isn't working.

- Patients come to you because they want more from their life. They want an increase in their performance and want to continue to feel and look great.

- Patients sometimes feel out of control and fear further loss, especially when a condition has persisted. They want you to help them get back in control of their health.

- Patients want to be happy, and their condition or circumstance is interfering with feeling happy.

- Most people are able and willing to pay for the things they want, but not always for the things they need.

The Challenge

The problem with most patient interactions is that they fail to get results for the patient. Allow me to repeat that statement. They fail to get results for the patient. Most interactions do not cultivate trust, deliver meaning, or move the patient to follow through. Reports and day-to-day dialogues too often leave the patient dazed and confused because they are loaded with facts, fear, and force of words. While people may begin care, they rarely follow through. They quit at the first setback, frustration, or relief from their symptoms.

Let's look at the physiological challenge that you, your staff, and your patients experience during the adjustment. While focused on a task, the brain processes 110 bits of information per second, yet it takes a full 40 bits of processing capacity to hold a conversation with someone. In the clinical environment, your mental RAM capacity can be reached very rapidly.

Now add the distractions from hearing other conversations, the phone ringing, children crying, and noises from outside. How about the staff interruptions as they ask you, "When do you want to see Mary again?" or "Mr. Marks is here for his re-exam, but Shannon called in sick. Should we reschedule him?" With systems and training, you will eliminate these interruptions and minimize your mental fatigue.

Patients Need Logical Steps

You have, through personal experience and study, arrived at some very profound conclusions concerning the nature of health, healing, and disease, yet most of your patients have reached other conclusions. So you will need to be patient with them and provide tangible platforms to help them reach new, more useful conclusions.

Remember, someone was patient with you. You did not come to these conclusions in a vacuum of self-study and reflection. Someone or some event influenced you and shifted your perspective. Somebody is still patiently prodding you to higher revelations.

Look with a beginner's mind and get back in touch with your "aha" moments. Strive to find new ways to demonstrate and explain to other beginners the logical reasons and experiences that helped you arrive at your conclusion.

A trusted and proven medium for teaching is to use analogies. People prefer the familiar, and when you use analogies, you are accelerating the learning process by connecting something familiar to a new idea. It gives a tangible feel to our abstract ideas. A few key points on analogies:

- Relate to their occupation
- Relate to their hobbies
- Relate to their educational experiences
- Use universally familiar items and experiences

You must relate to patients in the language and style they need. Some people need more information, some less. Some people need you to be more linear and logical, and others just want the bottom line with few details. Some of your patients want you to be friendly and contactable. Others want you to keep your distance. Did you know that only 8 percent of your patients need detailed care plans?

Peter resurfaced two years later. He seemed to be changed—a much more cooperative man. In reality, he hadn't changed at all. It was I. Now that my staff and I understood behavioral styles, we realized that Peter was a bottom-line, no-fluff kind of guy. So we stopped looking for warm, fuzzy validations from him and got right to the point. As a team, we learned to communicate so effectively that he wanted the care he needed. And of course, he paid my full fee and referred church members like crazy.

As I write this book, health reform has passed in the United States, yet the controversy continues. Whether there is real reform or not remains to be seen. I hope that we will be able to set aside our partisan views and bring the patient to the center of the discussion. Similar discussions are taking place worldwide as chiropractic utilization is growing. As we have discussed, your job is to make certain that your business thrives in all environments. Your future depends upon your ability to take care of more people with limited resources in a challenging health-care market.

Through the years, independent surveys conclude that chiropractors, just like you, rank high in patient satisfaction. Yet what got us here will not be enough. We cannot sit on this lead. Now that we are mainstream health-care providers, we have an opportunity to set the bar even higher.

Applying the E-Myth principles to my practice and having done the work you are doing has set us free to serve people better than any business in our community.

To what category of patient are you most drawn? A tactile patient for whom people are most important? A neutral patient for whom the mechanics of how you practice chiropractic is most important? An experimental patient for whom cutting-edge innovation is important? A traditional patient for whom low cost and certainty of delivery are absolutely essential?

Once you've defined your ideal patients, go after them. There's no reason you can't attract these types of people to your chiropractic practice and give them exactly what they want. Now let's get the next piece of the puzzle as Michael talks about growth. ✤

CHAPTER 17

On the Subject
of Growth

Michael E. Gerber

Growth is the only evidence of life.

—John Henry Newman, *Apologia Pro Vita Sua*

The rule of business growth says that every business, like every child, is destined to grow. Needs to grow. Is determined to grow.

Once you've created your chiropractic practice, once you've shaped the idea of it, the most natural thing for it to do is to . . . *grow!* And if you stop it from growing, it will die.

Once a chiropractor has started a practice, it's his or her job to help it grow. To nurture it and support it in every way. To infuse it with

- purpose;
- passion;
- will;
- belief;
- personality; and
- method.

As your practice grows, it naturally changes. And as it changes from a small practice to something much bigger, you will begin to feel out of control. News flash: that's because you *are* out of control.

Your practice *has* exceeded your know-how, sprinted right past you, and now it's taunting you to keep up. That leaves you two choices: grow as big as your practice demands you grow, or try to hold your practice at its present level—at the level you feel most comfortable.

The sad fact is that most chiropractors do the latter. They try to keep their practice small, securely within their comfort zone. Doing what they know how to do, what they feel most comfortable doing. It's called playing it safe.

But as the practice grows, the number, scale, and complexity of tasks will grow, too, until they threaten to overwhelm the chiropractor. More people are needed. More space. More money. Everything seems to be happening at the same time. A hundred balls are in the air at once.

As I've said throughout this book: Most chiropractors are not entrepreneurs. They aren't true businesspeople at all, but technicians suffering from an entrepreneurial seizure. Their philosophy of coping with the workload can be summarized as "just do it," rather than figuring out how to get it done through other people using innovative systems to produce consistent results.

Given most chiropractors' inclination to be the master juggler in their practice, it's not surprising that as complexity increases, as work expands beyond their ability to do it, as money becomes more elusive, they are just holding on, desperately juggling more and more balls. In the end, most collapse under the strain.

You can't expect your practice to stand still. You can't expect your practice to stay small. A practice that stays small and depends on you to do everything isn't a practice—it's a job!

Yes, just like your children, your business must be allowed to grow, to flourish, to change, to become more than it is. In this way, it will match your vision. And you know all about vision, right? You'd better. It's what you do best!

Do you feel the excitement? You should. After all, you know what your practice *is* but not what it *can be*.

It's either going to grow or die. The choice is yours, but it is a choice that must be made. If you sit back and wait for change to overtake you, you will always have to answer no to this question: Are you ready?

This brings us to the subject of *change*. But first, let's listen to what Dr. Frank has to say about growth. ✤

CHAPTER 18

Growth Meets Arrested Development

Dr. Frank Sovinsky

If we're growing, we're always going to be out of our comfort zone.

—John Maxwell

Now it's time for full disclosure. The whole time you have been reading this book, an "E-Virus" has been erasing most of your chiropractor-as-employee files. You are beginning to think like an entrepreneur thinks, and soon you will be ready to act like an entrepreneur acts. The technician's seizure is quieting. But we have a few more programs to install.

Michael makes the analogy that a business naturally grows just like a child does. A new business grows from its infancy stage through adolescence and expands to maturity. The genius of this observation is that it doesn't take an MBA to figure out why most chiropractic practices don't work.

Now get ready for this one. Unless you just started your practice, you are as busy as you can be. Your mental RAM is operating at capacity from doing it, doing it, doing it, and your systems are not adequate to support and sustain maturity. And the number one reason a practice doesn't work (drum roll please) is that doctors need to be in control.

Your practice is meeting a very specific need in your community because you have skills that meet those needs. That is the practice's purpose for being in existence. If you have done your demographic analysis and have concluded that you have enough people in your community to do business with, then the only limiting factor is you.

Growth occurs as demand rises and your skill set increases. This skill set includes you and your chiropractic techs' clinical skills and soft skills, and the systematization of your practice.

You started with that one new patient, did a superb job, and that person told others. Now you have a room full of patients waiting to be seen, heard, and helped. The need is there, but does your skill set meet the demand? Is your business as competent as you are?

Your personal development and growth parallels your business's expansion or contraction. As a mentor and business advisor, I witness men and women growing as people, simply by letting their businesses run their natural course. They get comfortable with ambiguity and risk-taking. They wrestle with self-doubt and realize that it has no place in business. They keep their minds and hearts wide open as they allow more and more patients to experience chiropractic care.

Regardless of your current level of success, we invite you to expand. Compared to what is truly possible, what you have done up to this point is mediocre. I know that sounds harsh, but it is a compliment. It is a belief in you and your destiny.

Success is defined in the *Encarta Dictionary* as the achievement of something planned or attempted. Now's the time, and this is the place to make bigger plans and attempt far grander goals. Raise the bar. No, knock the dome off the sky.

Stretch to Grow

You have to experience a few stretch marks to reach your bench-marks. The E-Myth viewpoint is that your practice must allow its current systems to get stressed and even snap at times in order to grow. This is why the need to control and be comfortable chokes a practice. You have to let go to grow. Let me share a typical problem every practice experiences, yet very few solve.

Most practices stay stuck in the adolescence phase because they deny or fail to account for the 2.5 Rule. Like you, we have observed a simple yet profound reality. Your practice sees 60 to 70 percent of its patient volume in 2.5 hours each day.

On average this is the first thirty minutes in the morning, the first thirty minutes in the afternoon (back from lunch), and the last hour and a half in the early evening. Seasonal changes may affect the busy time slots, yet the rule is consistent.

Doctors attempt to get around this rule by adding hours to their day, days to their week, or try to force patients to schedule appointments during their slower hours. In the financial analysis, numbers don't lie. This strategy does not work. The contraction phase begins, and the expansion momentum is annihilated. But at least you're in control, right? Wrong!

After years of personal experience and precise analysis of practices worldwide, we have another psychographic pearl to share with you. It is a big one, so hold it to the light. Chiropractic patients have preferred appointment times, and they expect you to accommodate them.

The patient preferred times are 5:30 a.m. to 8:00 a.m. (before work), 11:00 a.m. to 1:00 p.m. (lunch), and 4:30 p.m. to 6:30 p.m. (after work).

If you have been around Michael's E-Myth revolution long, you have come to appreciate why he admires McDonald's. I know why.

McDonald's customers have preferred times, too. Walk into one at 12:30 p.m. and you'll see it packed with patrons, all of the employees have their smiles on, and they're helping customers get in, get what they came for, and get out. But if you walk in at 11:00 a.m., the place is never busy. Staff are standing around at the registers, waiting. No one wants to eat lunch or breakfast at this time.

Like McDonald's, your systems must be able to accommodate the bulk of your patients during the preferred times. If you want to see fifty patients a day, you won't be seeing six people each hour, one every ten minutes, spread equally over eight hours.

First of all, that won't work because you can't control people, and some will come early, others will be late, and a few will actually play by your rules and arrive on time. But mainly it won't work because 60 to 70 percent of those fifty patients, that's about thirty-two, are going to want to come during the 2.5 busiest hours of your day. That's actually about thirteen each hour.

Your systems must be able to deliver impeccable care and service to thirty-two people in 2.5 hours if you want to grow to serve fifty patients a day. Like McDonald's, there might not be anyone in your office at 11:00 a.m., but come 5:30 a.m., you're hopping. It's all about preferred times.

Your Need for Control Is a Costly Habit

The natural growth cycle gets stunted when the technician is in charge. The technician/clinician wants to be perfect and has a fuzzy definition for what great care is. The reality is he or she just wants to be comfortable and take care of patients. The technician loves adjusting, teaching, and solving difficult cases. But what about the business plan, the stakeholders, and your vision? Stay awake, entrepreneur, or else the technician will ruin it for everyone.

When the pressure is on, the technician refuses to listen to the other personalities the E-Myth describes. The manager is ignored, and the entrepreneur is silenced. The technician has caught his tail. Now what?

It's so hilarious to watch a dog obsessed with chasing his tail. Round and round he goes, growling, barking, and then he's got it.

Now what? Watching grown men and women perform the same dance is not as much fun.

As a mentor and business advisor, I watch client after client chase their tails. They are, of course, unaware of the futility of such an activity. Yet all of them feel the effects of the ferocious bite we call self-sabotage.

Self-sabotage is how people resolve the tension and pain surrounding the fear of success. Yes, you read that correctly, fear of success. When I first heard that people could actually be afraid of the one thing they were chasing, I thought it was a load of new-age crap. Once again I was wrong.

Can you think of a time when your months of hard work started to pay off? Remember how fired up you were? You just had your best day, your best week, and the best month in your career.

But then a sinking, nauseous feeling takes over. You begin to feel uncomfortable for no good reason. You begin to hear those nasty voices, "This can't last," or "Who am I kidding?" or "I don't really deserve this."

Fear that you can't keep it together, that someone will discover that you're really not that good or that your service is not up to a high enough standard. Fear fuels the need to get in control.

You go back to familiar habits. You're once again trapped by your arrested development. So what do you do? You do what you have learned to do when threatened or not comfortable. You seek, no, you demand control.

You tell yourself, "I don't know why I feel like this. I think I just need to back off a little until I get my bearings." The diversion is complete, the pressure is off.

Your need for control is a costly habit. Control is an illusion. It doesn't exist in the real world, only in yours. No one is ever in control. The need for control consumes lives. It strains and even destroys relationships, and it kills dreams. Fear drives the need for control.

The world is moving at a furious pace, and it is designed to reward those who are willing and able to match it stride for stride and then pick up the pace.

Will you be pushed along by chance, or will you choose to take charge? Will you be the driver or settle for the back of the bus?

This book is not a survival guide or an inspirational sonnet. This is your destiny commanding you to get on with it. Are you ready for the next upgrade? I know I am. So let's see what Michael has to say about that six-letter word, change. ✤

CHAPTER 19

On the Subject
of Change

Michael E. Gerber

There is nothing permanent except change.
—Heraclitus of Ephesus, *Lives of the Philosophers*

So your practice is growing. That means, of course, that it's also changing. Which means it's driving you and everyone in your life crazy.

That's because, to most people, change is a diabolical thing. Tell most people they've got to change, and their first instinct is to crawl into a hole. Nothing threatens their existence more than change. Nothing cements their resistance more than change. Nothing.

Yet for the past thirty-five years, that's exactly what I've been proposing to small business owners: the need to change. Not for the sake of change itself, but for the sake of their lives.

I've talked to countless chiropractors whose hopes weren't being realized through their practice; whose lives were consumed by work; who slaved increasingly longer hours for decreasing pay;

whose dissatisfaction grew as their enjoyment shriveled; whose practice had become the worst job in the world; whose money was out of control; whose employees were a source of never-ending hassles, just like their patients, their bank, and, increasingly, even their families.

More and more, these chiropractors spent their time alone, dreading the unknown and anxious about the future. And even when they were with people, they didn't know how to relax. Their mind was always on the job. They were distracted by work, by the thought of work. By the fear of falling behind.

And yet, when confronted with their condition and offered an alternative, most of the same chiropractors strenuously resisted. They assumed that if there were a better way of doing business, they already would have figured it out. They derived comfort from knowing what they believed they already knew. They accepted the limitations of being a chiropractor; or the truth about people; or the limitations of what they could expect from their patients, their employees, their associate chiropractors, their bankers—even their family and friends.

In short, most chiropractors I've met over the years would rather live with the frustrations they already have than risk enduring new frustrations.

Isn't that true of most people you know? Rather than opening up to the infinite number of possibilities life offers, they prefer to shut their life down to respectable limits. After all, isn't that the most reasonable way to live?

I think not. I think we must learn to let go. I think that if you fail to embrace change, it will inevitably destroy you.

Conversely, by opening yourself to change, you give your chiropractic practice the opportunity to get the most from your talents.

Let me share with you an original way to think about change, about life, about who we are and what we do. About the stunning notion of expansion and contraction.

Contraction versus Expansion

"Our salvation," a wise man once said, "is to allow." That is, to be open, to let go of our beliefs, to change. Only then can we move from a point of view to a viewing point.

That wise man was Thaddeus Golas, the author of a small, powerful book entitled *The Lazy Man's Guide to Enlightenment* (Seed Center, 1971).

Among the many inspirational things he had to say was this compelling idea:

> *The basic function of each being is expanding and contracting. Expanded beings are permeative; contracted beings are dense and impermeative. Therefore each of us, alone or in combination, may appear as space, energy, or mass, depending on the ratio of expansion to contraction chosen, and what kind of vibrations each of us expresses by alternating expansion and contraction. Each being controls his own vibrations.*

In other words, Golas tells us that the entire mystery of life can be summed up in two words: *expansion* and *contraction*. He goes on to say:

> *We experience expansion as awareness, comprehension, understanding, or whatever we wish to call it.*
>
> *When we are completely expanded, we have a feeling of total awareness, of being one with all life.*
>
> *At that level we have no resistance to any vibrations or inter-actions of other beings. It is timeless bliss, with unlimited choice of consciousness, perception, and feeling.*
>
> *When a [human] being is totally contracted, he is a mass particle, completely imploded.*
>
> *To the degree that he is contracted, a being is unable to be in the same space with others, so contraction is felt as fear, pain, unconsciousness, ignorance, hatred, evil, and a whole host of strange feelings.*

At an extreme [of contraction, a human being] has the feeling of being completely insane, of resisting everyone and everything, of being unable to choose the content of his consciousness.

Of course, these are just the feelings appropriate to mass vibration levels, and he can get out of them at any time by expanding, by letting go of all resistance to what he thinks, sees, or feels.

Stay with me here. Because what Golas says is profoundly important. When you're feeling oppressed, overwhelmed, exhausted by more than you can control—contracted, as Golas puts it—you can change your state to one of expansion.

According to Golas, the more contracted we are, the more threatened by change; the more expanded we are, the more open to change.

In our most enlightened—that is, open—state, change is as welcome as non-change. Everything is perceived as a part of ourselves. There is no inside or outside. Everything is one thing. Our sense of isolation is transformed to a feeling of ease, of light, of joyful relationship with everything.

As infants, we didn't even think of change in the same way, because we lived those first days in an unthreatened state. Insensitive to the threat of loss, most young children are only aware of *what is*. Change is simply another form of *what is*. Change just *is*.

However, when we are in our most contracted—that is, closed—state, change is the most extreme threat. If the known is what I have, then the unknown must be what threatens to take away what I have. Change, then, is the unknown. And the unknown is fear. It's like being between trapezes.

- To the fearful, change is threatening because things may get worse.
- To the hopeful, change is encouraging because things may get better.
- To the confident, change is inspiring because the challenge exists to improve things.

If you are fearful, you see difficulties in every opportunity. If you are fear-free, you see opportunities in every difficulty.

Fear protects what I have from being taken away. But it also disconnects me from the rest of the world. In other words, fear keeps me separate and alone.

Here's the exciting part of Golas's message: with this new understanding of contraction and expansion, we can become completely attuned to where we are at all times.

If I am afraid, suspicious, skeptical, and resistant, I am in a contracted state. If I am joyful, open, interested, and willing, I am in an expanded state. Just knowing this puts me on an expanded path. Always remembering this, Golas says, brings enlightenment, which opens me even more.

Such openness gives me the ability to freely access my options. And taking advantage of options is the best part of change. Just as there are infinite ways to greet a patient, there are infinite ways to run your practice. If you believe Thaddeus Golas, your most exciting option is to be open to all of them.

Because your life is lived on a continuum between the most contracted and most expanded—the most closed and most open— states, change is best understood as the movement from one to the other, and back again.

Most small business owners I've met see change as a thing in itself, as something that just happens to them. Most experience change as a threat. Whenever change shows up at the door, they quickly slam it. Many bolt the door and pile up the furniture. Some even run for their gun.

Few of them understand that change isn't a thing in itself, but rather the manifestation of many things. You might call it the revelation of all possibilities. Think of it as the ability at any moment to sacrifice what we are for what we could become.

Change can either challenge us or threaten us. It's our choice. Our attitude toward change can either pave the way to success or throw up a roadblock.

Change is where opportunity lives. Without change we would stay exactly as we are. The universe would be frozen still. Time would end.

At any given moment, we are somewhere on the path between a contracted and expanded state. Most of us are in the middle of the journey, neither totally closed nor totally open. According to Golas, change is our movement from one place in the middle toward one of the two ends.

Do you want to move toward contraction or toward enlightenment? Because without change, you are hopelessly stuck with what you've got.

Without change,

- we have no hope;
- we cannot know true joy;
- we will not get better; and
- we will continue to focus exclusively on what we have and the threat of losing it.

All of this negativity contracts us even more, until, at the extreme closed end of the spectrum, we become a black hole so dense that no light can get in or out.

Sadly, the harder we try to hold on to what we've got, the less able we are to do so. So we try still harder, which eventually drags us even deeper into the black hole of contraction.

Are you like that? Do you know anybody who is?

Think of change as the movement between where we are and where we're not. That leaves only two directions for change: either moving forward or slipping backward. We become either more contracted or more expanded.

The next step is to link change to how we feel. If we feel afraid, change is dragging us backward. If we feel open, change is pushing us forward.

Change is not a thing in itself, but a movement of our consciousness. By tuning in, by paying attention, we get clues to the state of our being.

Change, then, is not an outcome or something to be acquired. Change is a shift of our consciousness, of our being, of our humanity, of our attention, of our relationship with all other beings in the universe.

We are either "more in relationship" or "less in relationship." Change is the movement in either of those directions. The exciting part is that *we possess the ability to decide which way we go . . . and to know, in the moment, which way we're moving.*

Closed, open . . . Open, closed. Two directions in the universe. The choice is yours.

Do you see the profound opportunity available to you? What an extraordinary way to live!

Enlightenment is not reserved for the sainted. Rather, it comes to us as we become more sensitive to ourselves. Eventually, we become our own guides, alerting ourselves to our state, moment by moment: *open . . . closed . . . open . . . closed.*

Listen to your inner voice, your ally, and feel what it's like to be open and closed. Experience the instant of choice in both directions.

You will feel the awareness growing. It may be only a flash at first, so be alert. This feeling is accessible, but only if you avoid the black hole of contraction.

Are you afraid that you're totally contracted? Don't be—it's doubtful. The fact that you're still reading this book suggests that you're moving in the opposite direction.

You're more like a running back seeking the open field. You can see the opportunity gleaming in the distance. In the open direction.

Understand that I'm not saying that change itself is a point on the path; rather, it's the all-important movement.

Change is *in you,* not *out there.*

What path are you on? The path of liberation? Or the path of crystallization?

As we know, change can be for the better or for the worse.

If change is happening *inside* of you, it is for the worse only if you remain closed to it. The key, then, is your attitude—your acceptance or rejection of change. Change can be for the better only if you accept it. And it will certainly be for the worse if you don't.

Remember, change is nothing in itself. Without you, change doesn't exist. Change is happening inside of each of us, giving us clues to where we are at any point in time.

Rejoice in change, for it's a sign you are alive.

Are we open? Are we closed? If we're open, good things are bound to happen. If we're closed, things will only get worse.

According to Golas, it's as simple as that. Whatever happens defines where we are. *How* we are is *where* we are. It cannot be any other way.

For change is life.

Charles Darwin wrote, "It is not the strongest of the species that survive, nor the most intelligent, but the one that proves itself most responsive to change."

The growth of your chiropractic practice, then, is its change. Your role is to go with it, to be with it, to share the joy, embrace the opportunities, meet the challenges, learn the lessons.

Remember, there are three kinds of people: (1) those who make things happen, (2) those who let things happen, and (3) those who wonder what the hell happened. The people who make things happen are masters of change. The other two are its victims.

Which type are you?

The Big Change

If all this is going to mean anything to the life of your practice, you have to know when you're going to leave it. At what point, in your practice's rise from where it is now to where it can ultimately grow, are you going to sell it? Because if you don't have a clear picture of when you want out, your practice is the master of your destiny, not the reverse.

As we stated earlier, the most valuable form of money is equity, and unless your business vision includes your equity and how you will use it to your advantage, you will forever be consumed by your practice.

Your practice is potentially the best friend you ever had. It is your practice's nature to serve you, so let it. If, however, you are not a wise steward, if you do not tell your practice what you expect from it, it will run rampant, abuse you, use you, and confuse you.

Change. Growth. Equity.

Focus on the point in the future when you will take leave of your practice. Now reconsider your goals in that context. Be specific. Write them down.

Skipping this step is like tiptoeing through earthquake country. Who can say where the fault lies waiting? And who knows exactly when your whole world may come crashing down around you?

Which brings us to the subject of *time*. But first, let's listen to what Dr. Frank has to say about change. ✤

CHAPTER 20

Keep the Change

Dr. Frank Sovinsky

If you focus on results you will never change. If you focus on change you will get results.

—Jack Davis

Well, that last chapter was pretty heavy, don't you agree? I could almost hear your inside voice protesting, "I thought this was a business book, not a philosophical treatise." Then you settled into the rhythm of those powerful words and realized that your business is a reflection of your philosophy concerning life. The thing is, most of us never take the time to think about our lives. We are too busy working in our practice.

My office was in the northern San Joaquin Valley in California. One day as I drove by a field of farm laborers bent over hoeing the tomatoes, I stopped my car and watched. The workers never looked up. They stayed in their rows doing it, doing the thing they were paid to do. I suspect that each day was more of the same, just a different row, different field, different crop, hard work, little time to think.

When I went back to the office, I had one of those moments where I was the observer of my life. Do you know what I mean? It was weirdly wonderful. I felt as if I were standing outside my body looking at my adjusting rituals. There I was, going from room to room, table to table, row to row. I was suffering from "presenteeism"—my body was there, but my mind was somewhere else. That's working in your business, and I don't want you to end up like that. And if you already are, I want to wake you from your day-mare. Are you ready? Here it comes.

Change is not a choice. Sameness is an illusion. I really don't know how we could ever imagine that we can avoid change. Your body is changing right inside of you, and you are hurtling through this solar system. Your mind is changing with every word you read.

I know we resist change, resent it, and ultimately fail to respond and take charge of the changes in our life. But really, why must we waste so much time trying to keep things the same?

Get with the program. Life happens with or without your approval.

One thing I know for sure is this: Your practice is in a constant state of flux, whether you are aware of it or not. It is either moving toward or away from the equity goal line in any given quarter. You can take charge of that if you want to.

So with all this talk about change, who needs it? You do. When you consciously and with deliberate effort change your thinking, you will change your behavior and change the results you are getting.

If you hear that inner voice saying, "Compared to most people, I am doing pretty well," take a look around. You might be the big fish in your pond, but there is a whole ocean of possibilities. A goldfish grows to the size of its bowl—bigger bowl, bigger fish; open water, really big fish. Think outside the bowl.

We are a goal-seeking species with a genetic code primed to be expressed. This code can be unlocked with a simple shift in your attitude. Here it is—are you ready? It's time to openly express your dissatisfaction with your life as it is. I know that sounds negative. It's not. It's a positive commitment to be the best and forget the rest.

Go ahead, say it out loud: "I want more than this." Now don't whine, just say it with strong conviction. "I want more than this." It may feel uncomfortable at first because we are taught to go with the flow and be content. Well, it's not natural.

This timid mindset has been bred into our psyche over generations in order to domesticate us. The cage has no lock and no kennel master. Simply walk out and be free. You were born to be free, to dream, and to create abundance.

Contraction Is a Choice

When I first meet new clients who are struggling, I tell them that their practice and their life is exactly the way they want it to be. They don't want to hear that, and so I continue. "You have what you have because you don't want to do what it takes to change." Their response is predictable and irrational. "I don't know how to change. I'm really confused about what I should do."

What they are really saying is, "I don't know how to change and still be comfortable. I don't know how to change and still be in control. I don't know how to change without taking a risk." There is no solution for that dilemma, just as there is no right answer to the wrong question. The next time you tell yourself that you are confused, stop and ask, "What am I pretending not to know?"

I admit that conscious change is uncomfortable, risky, and painful at times, but regret is far worse than any of the fleeting pain you might experience. Life is too long to live in obscurity and mediocrity.

I have another question for you. How long does it take to change? Twenty-one days? Two years? Seven years?

Are you ready for this? Change is instantaneous. Change is now. Change happens at the speed of thought. It can happen as you read this paragraph. Do you know why it seems to take so long? Making the decision to change takes time. It can drag out for days, months, and years. This is one reason decision making is so important to a chiropractic entrepreneur.

We all get stuck on different things. Some of our clients take a year or more to change their clinic hours; others do it in weeks.

Some anguish over fee changes for months; others make an imme-diate change. While the fears surrounding the thoughts of change are universal, the rationalizations for keeping things as they are get quite imaginative. Yet the result is always the same. Nothing gets better because nothing changes.

While there is merit in the tried and true in times of rapid change, such procedures and beliefs are dysfunctional at best. This is a time of rapid change!

As a mentor I have witnessed the absolute freedom that clients earn once they *get it.* What is *it?* It is the deep understanding that change is an action, not a thought. Change is work, not a plan. Change is an event, not a process. Change *who* you are while you change *how* you do things.

Decision Making

You make decisions all day long that affect the health of your patients. It's hard work, and you're good at it. You have settled into a decision-making process for those choices and changes that need to occur. Now it's time to expand that capacity to your practice.

Indecision is the only decision that is doomed to fail. When deciding on a course of action, whether it is hiring a staff, a coach, or changing your business model, ask a simple question: "Will doing this move me closer to or further away from my goal?" Most of your choices are pretty simple.

Make certain that you get the business plan straight in your head. Share it with someone who will hold you accountable. A competent plan will give you the confidence to make the changes.

Yet I must tell you, no plan is perfect. You may find that as you innovate, you will need to make changes to your plan. As Mike Tyson put it, "Everyone has a plan—until they get punched in the face."

Free Will and Free Won't

You have heard Michael talk about how most people are sleepwalkers who just go through the motions, and that we must do everything possible to wake up and stay awake. But do you get that he is talking about you and me? Ouch! I mention this because change means you will have to make fully conscious decisions from this point forward in spite of your neurobiology. Let me explain.

You know about free will, but what do you know about "free won't?" Every day your brain is bombarded by tens of thousands of chunks of information. Information that must be identified, sorted, prioritized, and acted upon. So who is making the choices, you or your brain? On a simple level, free will and free won't choices involve acting on impulse. I'll share a personal one.

Today is a gorgeous day at Lake Tahoe. It's sunny and warm, and the water is a deep cobalt blue. I want to go outside to the dock and get on my boat. My mind tells my body how great it would feel. My thoughts begin to build and reinforce the impulse to hit the water. Now choice and discipline enter. I know that if I stay home instead of going on my boat, I can finish this book sooner. I can hear the other voice telling me that I need a break and that this would be good for my creativity. Will I stay or will I go? Do I really have a choice, or has it already been decided for me?

So here's an interesting question: What are you going to do after you finish reading this section? You may not know that yet, but your brain probably does.

A study reported in *Scientific American Mind* in September 2009 shows that patterns of brain activity can reveal which choice a person is going to make long before he or she is aware of it. A team led by John-Dylan Haynes of the Bernstein Center for Computational Neuroscience Berlin scanned the brains of volunteers who held a button in each hand and were told to push one of the buttons whenever they wanted to. The scientist could tell from the scans which hand participants were going to use as early as ten seconds before the volunteers were aware that they made up their mind.

This study is the first to show unconscious predictive activity in a region associated with decision-making—the prefrontal cortex. The results support the notion that unconscious brain activity comes first and conscious activity follows as a result.

So what does this mean? There are a host of competing arguments about how much control we actually have in our day-to-day lives. Some believe that our brain simply reacts to stimulation and our body acts independent of our will. Others believe that every act we take began as a divine movement and is predetermined. While debate rages, you and I need a working theory that will give us traction in our climb to the summit.

Thoughts alone do not move the universe, but your thoughts move you to speak, to act, and to be attracted to resources and opportunities that will get you to the next step in your career. While it is clear that we do not have control over the thoughts that pop into our head, we can take charge once we are aware of them. We choose to feed or starve them. That's power.

Focus On the Life You Want, Not the Life You Want To Avoid

If you want success, stop planning for failure. Stop wasting your time worrying about the things that could go wrong and the obstacles you face. Stop majoring in the minors. It is your focus that gives adversity power over you. Needless struggle brought to you by you.

We always move toward our most dominant thoughts and often create the very situations we want to avoid. And because we are focused on protecting the back door, we miss opportunities coming through the front door. Obsessing about what others will think about all the changes you are making is guaranteed to attract failure.

Most of the battles that you fight will never happen. They exist only in your mind. The battle of the "what ifs" is not a battle of wits, it is an emotional carjacking. "What if I don't have the right plan? What if I don't have what it takes? What if my patients don't like it?"

Worry and anxiety are fear-driven behaviors that drain the mental resources you need to build a practice that works. Worry is negative goal-setting.

You have a choice whether or not you tune into these thoughts and amplify the misery, or simply pull your attention toward the life you want. All of these voices and thought attacks can be quieted by being more decisive, which means trust and faith in the process, and that means letting go.

Successful people leave this mental battlefield with no wounds because they are disciplined. As soon as they recognize the "what if" battle cries, they seek the high ground, the place of possibilities. They know that the moment they shift their attention onto the next task that needs completing or skill that needs mastering, the battle vanishes.

It's not that they don't hit walls or get knocked off course. They face problems and have setbacks, yet they choose to look for solutions, not sympathy.

Innovation Is Intelligent Change

Remember when Michael said these three words: change, growth, and equity? He outlined a natural order, a destiny if you will. It begins with change. I want to share how innovation can be intelligent change, and how it will move you faster and further than you could have ever imagined.

Innovation is a deliberate act. It is intelligent because you are predicting the future. Innovation includes adding and letting go. Whether you add an entirely new system or a procedure within a current system, the thinking behind the change makes it intelligent.

As new ideas and methods of doing things are implemented, you will need to make sure they are congruent with your business plan and prioritized to assure successful outcomes. As Michael said, small business owners need to change, "Not for the sake of change itself, but for the sake of their lives."

The benefits of innovation on your practice are

- better personal results and greater socioeconomic impact;
- a more dynamic business with economic resiliency; and
- improved mental concentration, purposeful passion, and fulfillment.

Innovations have varying degrees of intensity.
First-degree innovation:

- Updating office décor
- Changing office hours
- Implementing new forms, procedures, and policies

Second-degree innovation:

- Remodeling your office
- Changing chiropractic techniques
- Recruiting, hiring, and training new staff
- Terminating a staff member

Third-degree innovation:

- Moving your office
- Starting a new practice
- Selling your practice

Each degree of innovation requires more mental, financial, and emotional resources to follow through with the innovation. The life of a chiropractic entrepreneur is rich with opportunities to grow.

Just Did It

Everyone wants to go to heaven, yet nobody wants to die. This is a disturbing metaphor for growing through to the next level. The brutal fact is this: in order to have the life you want, you will have to leave pieces of the life you have.

It's not what you add to your life that makes it extraordinary, it's what you let go of. That's right: you cannot move forward with one foot in the past and the other stretching into the future. Success cannot be achieved while thinking and acting as you have in the past.

In the beginning, you may find it challenging to escape the fear-tainted thoughts swirling around in your mind. The familiar—though it may be uncomfortable—is still predictable and appears safe. In stark contrast, change is unpredictable and fuels your anxiety.

Look, we want to be there when the doctor you are now meets the doctor you are destined to become. It will be a party. Yet we have a few more pixels to put in place, so let's see what Michael has to say about time. ✤

CHAPTER 21

On the Subject of Time

Michael E. Gerber

Take time to deliberate; but when the time for action arrives, stop thinking and go in.

—Andrew Jackson

"I'm running out of time!" chiropractors often lament. "I've got to learn how to manage my time more carefully!"

Of course, they see no real solution to this problem. They're just worrying the subject to death. Singing the chiropractor's blues.

Some make a real effort to control time. Maybe they go to time management classes, or faithfully try to record their activities during every hour of the day.

But it's hopeless. Even when chiropractors work harder, even when they keep precise records of their time, there's always a shortage of it. It's as if they're looking at a square clock in a round universe. Something doesn't fit. The result: the chiropractor is constantly chasing work, money, life.

And the reason is simple. Chiropractors don't see time for what it really is. They think of time with a small "t," rather than Time with a capital "T."

Yet Time is simply another word for *your life*. It's your ultimate asset, your gift at birth—and you can spend it any way you want. Do you know how you want to spend it? Do you have a plan?

How do *you* deal with Time? Are you even conscious of it? If you are, I bet you are constantly locked into either the future or the past. Relying on either memory or imagination.

Do you recognize these voices? "Once I get through this, I can have a drink . . . go on a vacation . . . retire." "I remember when I was young and practicing chiropractic was satisfying."

As you go to bed at midnight, are you thinking about waking up at 7:00 a.m. so that you can get to the office by 8:00 a.m. so that you can go to lunch by noon, because your software people will be there at 1:30 p.m. and you've got a full schedule and a new patient scheduled for 2:30 p.m.?

Most of us are prisoners of the future or the past. While pinballing between the two, we miss the richest moments of our life—the present. Trapped forever in memory or imagination, we are strangers to the here and now. Our future is nothing more than an extension of our past, and the present is merely the background.

It's sobering to think that right now each of us is at a precise spot somewhere between the beginning of our Time (our birth) and the end of our Time (our death). No wonder everyone frets about Time. What really terrifies us is that *we're using up our life and we can't stop it.*

It feels as if we're plummeting toward the end with nothing to break our free fall. Time is out of control! Understandably, this is horrifying, mostly because the real issue is not time with a small "t" but Death with a big "D."

From the depths of our existential anxiety, we try to put Time in a different perspective—all the while pretending we can manage it. We talk about Time as though it were something other than what it is. "Time is money," we announce, as though that explains it.

But what every chiropractor should know is that Time is life. And Time ends! Life ends!

The big, walloping, irresolvable problem is that *we don't know how much Time we have left.*

Do you feel the fear? Do you want to get over it?

Let's look at Time more seriously.

To fully grasp Time with a capital "T," you have to ask the big Question: *How do I wish to spend the rest of my Time?*

Because I can assure you that if you don't ask that big Question with a big "Q," you will forever be assailed by the little questions. You'll shrink the whole of your life to *this time* and *next time* and the *last time*—all the while wondering, *what time is it?*

It's like running around the deck of a sinking ship worrying about where you left the keys to your cabin.

You must accept that you have only so much Time; that you're using up that Time second by precious second. And that your Time, your life, is the most valuable asset you have. Of course, you can use your Time any way you want. But unless you choose to use it as richly, as rewardingly, as excitingly, as intelligently, as *intentionally* as possible, you'll squander it and fail to appreciate it.

Indeed, if you are oblivious to the value of your Time, you'll commit the single greatest sin: You will live your life unconscious of its passing you by.

Until you deal with Time with a capital "T," you'll worry about time with a small "t" until you have no Time—or life—left. Then your Time will be history . . . along with your life.

I can anticipate the question: If Time is the problem, why not just take on fewer patients? Well, that's certainly an option, but probably not necessary. I know a chiropractor with a small practice who sees four times as many patients as the average, yet the doctor and staff don't work long hours. How is it possible?

This chiropractor has a system. By using this expert system, the employees can do everything the chiropractor or his associate chiropractors would do—everything that isn't chiropractor-dependent.

Be versus Do

Remember when we all asked, "What do I want to be when I grow up?" It was one of our biggest concerns as children.

Notice that the question isn't, "What do I want to *do* when I grow up?" It's "What do I want to *be?*"

Shakespeare wrote, "To be or not to be." Not "To do or not to do."

But when you grow up, people always ask you, "What do you *do?*" How did the question change from *being* to *doing?* How did we miss the critical distinction between the two?

Even as children, we sensed the distinction. The real question we were asking was not what we would end up *doing* when we grew up, but who we would *be.*

We were talking about a *life* choice, not a *work* choice. We instinctively saw it as a matter of how we spend our Time, not what we do *in* time.

Look to children for guidance. I believe that as children we instinctively saw Time as life and tried to use it wisely. As children, we wanted to make a life choice, not a work choice. As children, we didn't know—or care—that work had to be done on time, on budget.

Until you see Time for what it really is—your life span—you will always ask the wrong question.

Until you embrace the whole of your Time and shape it accordingly, you will never be able to fully appreciate the moment.

Until you fully appreciate every second that comprises Time, you will never be sufficiently motivated to live those seconds fully.

Until you're sufficiently motivated to live those seconds fully, you will never see fit to change the way you are. You will never take the quality and sanctity of Time seriously.

And unless you take the sanctity of Time seriously, you will continue to struggle to catch up with something behind you. Your frustrations will mount as you try to snatch the second that just whisked by.

If you constantly fret about time with a small "t," then Time will blow right past you. And you'll miss the whole point, the real truth about Time: You can't manage it; you never could. You can only *live* it.

And so that leaves you with these questions: How do I live my life? How do I give significance to it? How can I be here now, in this moment?

Once you begin to ask these questions, you'll find yourself moving toward a much fuller, richer life. But if you continue to be caught up in the banal work you do every day, you're never going to find the time to take a deep breath, exhale, and be present in the now.

So, let's talk about the subject of *work*. But first, let's listen to what Dr. Frank has to say about time. ✤

CHAPTER 22

Stepping into Time

Dr. Frank Sovinsky

The future is something which everyone reaches at the rate of sixty minutes an hour, whatever he does, whoever he is.

—C.S. Lewis

How will you spend the rest of your lifetime? Sobering thought that we are somewhere in between birth and un-birth, isn't it? So let's make a deal that from this point forward we will invest our time and not just spend it.

We will invest in our life through passionate relationships.

We will invest in our life by having more fun.

We will invest in our life by taking time to dream.

We will invest in our life by taking action.

Why is it that successful doctors always have time to do the things that need to get done and struggling doctors never seem to have enough time? You guessed it, they have a system. They work smart and play hard!

Successful doctors have learned how to leverage their personal energy while managing their time, and you can too. Just like you, I have read many books with good suggestions on how to budget my time, yet none of them seemed to resonate with me. I needed more freedom, more flexibility, and a holistic viewpoint.

Words are potent predecessors of human potential. We use the words "energetic," "enthusiastic," and "inspiring" to describe entrepreneurs we admire. Let's assign those descriptions to you right now, and then your job is to step into them. Try a little potential on, see how it fits.

As a chiropractic entrepreneur, you need a source of renewable energy to work on the business while you are working in it. Juggling family life and running a flourishing practice, even with the right systems and people, still requires personal power.

The beautiful thing about being a chiropractic entrepreneur, aside from the awesome feeling we get as a result of helping our patients, is the freedom from long hours associated with other healing professions.

Tightly orchestrated systems and the right people doing the right things can set you free from the drudgery of industrial-age office hours, and let you step into the "peak performance time zone."

Work Smart, Play Hard

No single personal issue or practice-related challenge is insurmountable or life-draining. However, over the course of taking your practice through its growth cycle, the accumulative stress can drain your physical, mental, and emotional reserves.

Instinctively we know how to maintain enough energy for practice survival. Yet when it comes to thriving in practice, the energy demands are so massive that without a system, success is doubtful.

In keeping with the simplicity and power of the E-Myth management process of innovation, quantification, and orchestration, we at DC Mentors have designed a system that we call the "Rejuvenation System."

It has been tested, measured, and implemented in practices worldwide, and has helped sustain the transformation of doctors from employees to entrepreneurs.

The Rejuvenation System is personal energy management and time management together. This is the solution to finding time to work *on* your business while working *in* it, and give you time off for better behavior. Simply put: work smart, play hard.

Your personal energy is an unstable mixture of mental stamina, emotional strength, and physical power. Stabilizing this creative source of energy is essential if you are going to focus it. You need time to think, to work, and to play.

Time management is the procedure that organizes *when* the work of the practice takes place. It includes patient scheduling, tactical work hours, and strategic work sessions.

Let's look at this revolutionary approach to practice time management, and you will get a feel as to how it incorporates personal energy management along with it.

Got Rhythm?

In order to keep your promise to your patients, you need to deliver a consistent, quality clinical experience and high touch interactions. Your cognitive abilities must be highly tuned and your personal energy consistent. Personal energy puts cognition to work.

You and your team must be able to multitask flawlessly throughout the entire day, each and every day. Now let me make a point about multitasking. Emerging research suggests that we don't actually multitask. We switch attention from one task to the next. And this is why your cognitive endurance is critical to high performance.

Time, it seems, is both natural and artificial. Natural time includes the rhythms of our biological clocks, our life span, and the passage of this planet around the sun. Artificial time is the alarm clock, the time clock, and the calendar wristwatch.

We, of course, live in a world where we need to step into natural time and not be stepped on by artificial time. Here's the logic behind the Rejuvenation System's office hours.

The patient-preferred times that I described in chapter 18 are 5:30 a.m. to 8:00 a.m. (before work), 11:00 a.m. to 1:00 p.m. (lunch), and 4:30 p.m. to 6:30 p.m. (after work). A misplaced work ethic can lead to great effort and little reward. Clinics that try to capture all three peak times find it impossible to sustain mental and physical energy. The eventual result is burnout for the doctor and the chiropractic techs. The impact on the business is measurable. You only need to capture two peak demand times in order to grow.

The natural rhythms of our body have been described as the circadian rhythm and the ultradian rhythm.

Circadian Rhythm

Researchers have discovered that we have a circadian clock that is synchronized with cycles of light and dark and other factors such as ambient temperature, mealtimes, stress, and exercise.

The evidence suggests that most people experience their highest mental alertness at 10:00 a.m. DC Mentors clients begin seeing patients at 10:00 a.m. to take full advantage of their innate energy spikes.

The following points of reference demonstrate how to best use your performance cycle:

10:00 a.m.—highest mental alertness

2:30 p.m.—best coordination

3:30 p.m.—fastest reaction time

5:00 p.m.—greatest cardiovascular efficiency and muscle strength

Ultradian Rhythm

You probably recognize that you have periods of high and low energy throughout the day. These fluctuations are known as ultradian rhythms, one of the brain's many different cycles. They last about 90 to 110 minutes, so there are about twelve to sixteen cycles over a twenty-four-hour period. If you have a peak at 10:00 a.m., your low will occur about 45 minutes later. Your next peak of energy will occur at noon.

Your brain's rhythm plays a key role in understanding, and influences cognitive performance, memory processes, visual perception, levels of arousal and performance, mood, and behavior.

Toward the end of each cycle our bodies crave a period of recovery. But most of us override the urge because we are regimented by a mechanical clock, not our biological timing. The result is that we get tapped out physically and emotionally a little bit more each day.

Sure, we might be productive in the short run, but beware. Your body has a memory, and violations to its rhythm will not be tolerated without a physical or emotional warning, or worse, a crisis.

Here's a plan that works. You only need to manage three ultradian rhythms a day, one in the morning and two in the afternoon. Experiment with different nutrient-rich foods and beverages at the beginning of each rhythm, and especially when you may have to go back-to-back in the afternoon (pun intended).

Include a few stretches and even a three-minute music session with your MP3 player. You will be recharged, and your patients will get a much better experience. Remember, it's not about being good, it's about being remarkable day in, day out.

For more information on recommended clinic hours go to www. michaelegerber.com/co-author.

Time Off for Better Behavior

The Rejuvenation System even organizes your time off to sustain and renew your personal energy. Just like you, I love time off! I know that taking time off to recreate will keep me balanced and my business prosperous.

Now before you drop everything and take off, let's plan it! Most of you still have a job, and that means the chiropractor-as-employee either skips vacations or uses ineffective strategies such as week-long trips.

This old-practice thinking is ingrained in us as a result of our experiences while growing up. The once-a-year, "family fun" event was the thing we looked forward to the most. It worked for us then, but this is now.

We have proved that frequent mini-breaks are more effective and result in less momentum loss while building your practice.

I am going to share a few of our findings, and my advice is to apply them and see if you get the results our clients get.

Rule #1: Take time off before you need it.

Rule #2: Plan your time off.

Rule #3: Never skip them.

Take Time Off before You Need It

By the time you *need* a vacation, you are already too late. As with other physical signs of stress, the symptoms are the last signs to appear. It costs personal energy, vitality, and focus, and can cause economic downturns.

Waiting too long, or worse, never taking a break leads to the "Vacant Doc Syndrome." The lights are on, but nobody is home. This syndrome has many symptoms and signs. The doctor often describes it this way: "When I'm in the office, I feel like being somewhere else, and when I'm somewhere else, I can't stop worrying about the office." The doctor's physical shell shows up with a forced smile and anemic leadership attributes. The office turns into an asylum, and the inmates run it.

Plan Your Time Off

The frequency and duration of these timeout periods are so critical that deviating from them comes with a cost.

- We recommended that you take time off every eight weeks. That's six times a year!
- Four of these are shorter breaks that last three to four days (long weekends).
- The remaining two breaks can be extended stays lasting up to five days, including the weekend.

Never Skip Them

The most common reason doctors skip these breaks is that they fear losing momentum and losing their patients. With the right plan, neither will happen. It takes practice to learn how to take time off for better behavior. So get going.

Leisure Time

Now we need to manage that clock of yours when you're not in the office. You only have 960 minutes to get things done during an average day. Now before you check my math, I am subtracting 480 minutes for sleep. Please don't argue with your body and brain; they need it. Sleep deprivation stunts creativity.

Now once we subtract our clinic hours and the tactical work we need to do, we have "leisure time." This is when you have the most flexibility, so don't squander it. No matter how busy your life has become, you consume some amount of time during the week pursuing the following leisure activities: socializing, hobbies, sports, restaurants, and the Internet and other media (TV, movies, and reading).

Oddly enough, the Greek word for leisure is *schole*, and this is where we get the word school. When you first begin working on your business, you will need to eliminate a few current leisure activities and substitute ones that contribute directly to your "schooling."

You can take charge and invest your time wisely by drawing from this time and energy pool. Some examples:

- Listen to audiobooks while driving and exercising.
- Choose movies for their thought-provoking quality and artistic expression.
- Choose sports that require you to be in top physical condition (for example, basketball and soccer, not bowling).
- Hang out with entrepreneurs of like mind.
- Use the Internet for insight and education, not entertainment.
- Hire someone else to do routine maintenance work (lawn care, housework, fix-it chores).

Now before you close your ears, I realize that you are not me. For me, mowing my lawn was a distraction, not an attraction. Doing chores and fix-it jobs did not work for me. You may really enjoy doing those things, but at what cost? Is it truly contributing to the transformation, or is it a distraction from doing the work that must be done?

Remember in school when you knew you had to study for the national boards but instead you cleaned out a closet or washed the car? That's what I am talking to you about.

Now, my best friend and business partner tells me that some of the most profound times he has enjoyed with his children have been in the cab of his tractor mowing grass. No argument from me. That's the good life.

Think Outside the Box

We made a deal, you and I, at the beginning of the chapter. We agreed to invest our time, not just spend it. Watching television goes way beyond spending your time. It wastes your time! Turn it off, put it in another room, or sell it.

As a coach I am telling you to run this play if only for the time that it takes for your business plan to get traction in your practice. This could be a few months, it could be longer.

Instead of slumping in a chair, why not engage the real world with all of your senses, not the virtual reality of television? And that is what TV is, a "virtual reality." And don't get me started on the mindless drool of reality television programming. Is it any wonder why we are in such a climate of intellectual drought?

Think of the television you watch. Do the programs you watch in any way expose your mind to anything worthwhile? Do they move you closer to your goals in any way? If the answer is no, then stop it!

You can step into time and play this game from a whole new perspective. Invest your time, don't just spend it.

I know you are ready and willing, and soon you will be able to manifest that dream you have. Let's see what Michael has to teach us about work. ✤

CHAPTER 23

On the Subject of Work

Michael E. Gerber

As we learn we always change, and so our perception. This changed perception then becomes a new Teacher inside each of us.

—Hyemeyohsts Storm

In the business world, as the saying goes, the entrepreneur knows something about everything, the technician knows everything about something, and the switchboard operator just knows everything.

In a chiropractic practice, chiropractors see their natural work as the work of the technician. The Supreme Technician. Often to the exclusion of everything else.

After all, chiropractors get zero preparation working as a manager and spend no time thinking as an entrepreneur—those just aren't courses offered in today's schools and colleges of chiropractic. By the time they own their own chiropractic practice, they're just doing it, doing it, doing it.

At the same time, they want everything—freedom, respect, money. Most of all, they want to rid themselves of meddling bosses and start their own practice. That way they can be their own boss and take home all the money. These chiropractors are in the throes of an entrepreneurial seizure.

Chiropractors who have been praised for their ability to treat difficult cases or their extensive knowledge of natural health-care sciences believe they have what it takes to run a chiropractic practice. It's not unlike the plumber who becomes a contractor because he's a great plumber. Sure, he may be a great plumber . . . but it doesn't necessarily follow that he knows how to build a practice that does this work.

It's the same for a chiropractor. So many of them are surprised to wake up one morning and discover that they're nowhere near as equipped for owning their own practice as they thought they were.

More than any other subject, work is the cause of obsessive-compulsive behavior by chiropractors.

Work. You've got to do it every single day.

Work. If you fall behind, you'll pay for it.

Work. There's either too much or not enough.

So many chiropractors describe work as what they do when they're busy. Some discriminate between the work they *could* be doing as chiropractors and the work they *should* be doing as chiropractors.

But according to the E-Myth, they're exactly the same thing. The work you *could* do and the work you *should* do as a chiropractor are identical. Let me explain.

Strategic Work versus Tactical Work

Chiropractors can do only two kinds of work: strategic work and tactical work.

Tactical work is easier to understand, because it's what almost every chiropractor does almost every minute of every hour of every day. It's called getting the job done. It's called doing business.

Tactical work includes filing, billing, answering the telephone, going to the bank, and seeing patients.

The E-Myth says that tactical work is all the work chiropractors find themselves doing in a chiropractic practice to *avoid* doing the strategic work.

"I'm too busy," most chiropractors will tell you.

"How come nothing goes right unless I do it myself?" they complain in frustration.

Chiropractors say these things when they're up to their ears in tactical work. But most chiropractors don't understand that if they had done more strategic work, they would have less tactical work to do.

Chiropractors are doing strategic work when they ask the following questions:

- Why am I a chiropractor?
- What will my practice look like when it's done?
- What must my practice look, act, and feel like in order for it to compete successfully?
- What are the key indicators of my practice?

Please note that I said chiropractors *ask* these questions when they are doing strategic work. I didn't say these are the questions they necessarily answer.

That is the fundamental difference between strategic work and tactical work. Tactical work is all about *answers:* How to do this. How to do that.

Strategic work, in contrast, is all about *questions:* What practice are we really in? Why are we in that practice? Who specifically is our practice determined to serve? When will I sell this practice? How and where will this practice be doing business when I sell it? And so forth.

Not that strategic questions don't have answers. Chiropractors who commonly ask strategic questions know that once they ask such a question, they're already on their way to *envisioning* the answer. Question and answer are part of a whole. You can't find the right answer until you've asked the right question.

Tactical work is much easier, because the question is always more obvious. In fact, you don't ask the tactical question; instead, the question arises from a result you need to get or a problem you need to solve. Billing a patient is tactical work. Adjusting a patient is tactical work. Firing an employee is tactical work. Performing an interim exam is tactical work.

Tactical work is the stuff you do every day in your practice. Strategic work is the stuff you plan to do to create an exceptional practice/business/enterprise.

In tactical work, the question comes from *out there* rather than *in here*. The tactical question is about something *outside* of you, whereas the strategic question is about something *inside* of you.

The tactical question is about something you *need* to do, whereas the strategic question is about something you *want* to do. Want versus need.

If tactical work consumes you,

- you are always reacting to something outside of you;
- your practice runs you, you don't run it;
- your employees run you, you don't run them; and
- your life runs you, you don't run your life.

You must understand that the more strategic work you do, the more intentional your decisions, your practice, and your life become. *Intention* is the byword of strategic work.

Everything on the outside begins to serve you, to serve your vision, rather than forcing you to serve it. Everything you *need* to do is congruent with what you *want* to do. It means you have a vision, an aim, a purpose, a strategy, an *envisioned* result.

Strategic work is the work you do to *design* your practice, to design your life.

Tactical work is the work you do to *implement* the design created by strategic work.

Without strategic work, there is no design. Without strategic work, all that's left is keeping busy.

There's only one thing left to do. It's time to take action. But first, let's listen to what Dr. Frank has to say on the subject of work. ✤

CHAPTER 24

Work on the Life You Want, Not the Life You Want to Avoid

Dr. Frank Sovinsky

It is not enough to be busy; so are the ants. The question is: what are we busy about?

—Henry David Thoreau

My question for you is this: "What are you busy about?" In the previous chapter, Michael hit us with a few pithy ideas about work.

You must be "busy about" doing good work, both as the visionary strategist and the field tactician. Good work is effort that moves you toward personal fulfillment and destination success.

Strategic work is movement from inside out. It is the introspective grilling of our souls. No wonder so many choose to be busy ants and busy little worker bees and avoid it at all costs. But you are different. From the moment you began reading this book, you have been doing strategic work. Every question we have asked has been an invitation for you to create something that has never existed before you came into this world.

If you do the strategic work, the tactical work will be meaningful and get the results you are looking for. If you don't do the strategic work, you will end up doing busywork and will waste time doing the right things, but at the wrong times.

Strategic work sets you on a course toward the life you want, not the life you want to avoid. The most important question to ask is "Why am I a chiropractor?" Let the answers flow and you may find that your reason shifts and changes shape every so often. Some days it's "to get free," and on other days it's "to set people free."

The Strategic Triangle

Knowing what work needs to be done on any given day, week, or quarter is crucial. Without your business plan and a dynamic system to help you assess the practice's indicators, you miss out on the joy of work and the freedom it brings.

Allow me to introduce you to the *Strategic Triangle*, yet another powerful system that will help you close the gap between where your practice is now and where you want it to be. This real-time process is guaranteed to organize your strategic work so that it becomes a useful habit.

I want you to look at the next chart. The left side represents people's health-care needs, and the right side is your skill set. At the point the two sides meet is where you find the purpose for your business. People's needs and the skills that address those needs equal purpose. This triangle can serve as a useful visualization of how your practice can grow to maturity.

Now on the inside of the triangle we place three tiers: clinical competencies, soft skills, and business systems. This tiered platform will build a stronger, more resilient practice. Clinical competencies include patient-centered care and chiropractic technique mastery. The soft skills tier includes you and your staff's intrapersonal and interpersonal skills. Your practice's business systems tier includes new patient attraction, patient compliance, and patient fulfillment.

You will experience the next level of sustainable practice growth only when the Strategic Triangle expands. And that means that the three supportive tiers must grow simultaneously. The result is a mature business that can take care of more people, more efficiently, and with a higher level care and clinical effectiveness.

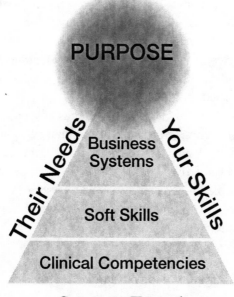

Strategic Triangle

This tiered supportive design implies a hierarchy with clinical competencies as the primary base and business systems at the top for good reason. Let me share a common example.

Dr. Jim is in a practice slump. He is convinced, after reading the trade journals, that his problem would be readily solved, once and for all, if he could just get some new patients in the door. He runs an ad or uses a public relations firm, and it works. New people come in, but because there are no systems in place to create office flow, it becomes a flood, drowning the practice in long wait times and substandard service experiences for both new and established patients.

The Strategic Triangle buckles under the top-heavy load. It cannot manage the increase in volume, and the practice's promise to the patient is not delivered. The perceived indifference, though unintentional, sends a message to Dr. Jim's subconscious and to his staff that being busier is no fun, and it sends a message to the community that Dr. Jim's practice doesn't work for them.

If you fail to see or use this hierarchy, you will do what all struggling business owners do when they are having an "out of money" experience or an "out of clients" experience. They seek the path of least resistance, the path of advertising and gimmicks to attract customers. And this is why their businesses go up and then spiral down. They missed the strategic work.

A mandate from all great business gurus falls on deaf ears, and I am afraid it is killing the dreams of too many chiropractors. The universal principle is simple: "Before you look at marketing, look at how your service is delivered." I told you it was simple. As in all get-rich-quick schemes, if it sounds too good to be true, it is. Be wary of "get-new-patient-rich" marketing schemes, because your reputation is your greatest asset.

Focusing Device for Tactical Work

Now that you have the Strategic Triangle in your short-term memory, we can use it as a focusing device for planning the tactical work that needs to be done. Use this device every day. Not just when you're in the mood or inspired.

When you're done reading today, I want you to get that drawing paper that you used in chapter 6 and draw the Strategic Triangle with the three supportive tiers. Put your drawing where you will be certain to see it in the morning and when you go to bed. Don't work on it tonight. Go to bed early. Get to sleep fast, and let the dream come. The mind does much of its best work when you don't try to control it.

Tomorrow morning get up early, even if you didn't sleep well. Once you're awake and have gone through your morning rituals, take out your favorite pen and touch the sides, top, and supportive tiers. Let your mind take you to a point of interest, and start making notes. Don't edit or look for the perfect words. Let go and reach in. It's not a Ouija board, it's just a focusing device.

In time, you will find that this can make your tactical work focused like a laser and not diffused like a spotlight. Let me share a couple of practical applications. Sometimes the more you question, the more you need to question, but I bet you already figured that out.

Tier 1, clinical competencies: What could I study today—technique, anatomy, research paper, Internet search for health-related news?

Tier 2, soft skills development: Is my vision clear, bright, and big? Am I proud of my business as it is? Do I love leading my team by my example? Do I look forward to training that new staff or correcting that veteran team member? Will I discipline my mood today? Am I going to be nice? Am I going to have fun and be fun to be around? How can I listen more and talk less? How can I paint a picture, deliver a phrase, or convey a feeling that sticks in the minds of my patients?

Tier 3, business systems: Go back to your business plan and to the work you have begun, and get those systems moving, get those systems humming. You've got to start systematizing your butt off!

Paper Time and Patient Time

You and your techs need to maintain a high level of present-time consciousness in order to shift your full attention from one person to the next, from one task to the next.

Distractions are costly. Research suggests that even a temporary shift from one task to another, like answering a phone call while checking your e-mail, can decrease your effectiveness by as much as 25 percent! So we need to install a system to prevent distractions.

At DC Mentors, our clients organize their time and tactical work into two categories, patient time and paper time. The crucial difference between patient time and paper time is where the techs and doctor focus their attention and energy.

Patient time is the time the doctor is scheduled to see patients. It's any time that a patient could be coming into the office to see the doctor. During patient time, we stop most administrative activities and focus on exceeding the patient's expectations.

Paper time is the part of the day when patients are not typically scheduled and the doctor may or may not be present in the office. This time is usually an hour or more in the morning before the doctor and patients arrive, and lunchtime. During paper time, the main focus is on the administrative responsibilities of running the business. This is the time to dictate your reports, train your staff, and hold meetings.

Patient-centered care is not a noun, it is an action verb. It means you cannot drift in and out of patient consciousness by engaging in any distracting activities. That means no phone calls, no e-mail or texting, and no playing on the Internet during patient time. You have to set a high standard, one that your team can believe in, and a lead they can follow.

You are doing good work right now, and I am proud of you! But hang in there; another piece of the puzzle is about to get put on the board. Let's see what Michael has to say about taking action. ✤

25

On the Subject of Taking Action

Michael E. Gerber

Deliberation is the work of many men. Action, of one alone.
—Charles de Gaulle

It's time to get started, time to take action. Time to stop thinking about the old practice and start thinking about the new practice. It's not a matter of coming up with better practices; it's about reinventing the practice of chiropractic.

And the chiropractor has to take personal responsibility for it.

That's you.

So sit up and pay attention!

You, the chiropractor, have to be interested. You cannot abdicate accountability for the practice of chiropractic, the administration of chiropractic, or the finance of chiropractic.

Although the goal is to create systems into which chiropractors can plug reasonably competent people—systems that allow the practice to run without them—chiropractors must take responsibility for that happening.

I can hear the chorus now: "But we're chiropractors! We shouldn't have to know about this." To that I say: whatever. If you don't give a flip about your practice, fine—close your mind to new knowledge and accountability. But if you want to succeed, then you'd better step up and take responsibility, and you'd better do it now.

All too often, chiropractors take no responsibility for the business of chiropractic but instead delegate tasks without any understanding of what it takes to do them; without any interest in what their people are actually doing; without any sense of what it feels like to be at the front desk when a patient comes in and has to wait for forty-five minutes; and without any appreciation for the entity that is creating their livelihood.

Chiropractors can open the portals of change in an instant. All you have to do is say, "I don't want to do it that way anymore." Saying it will begin to set you free—even though you don't yet understand what the practice will look like after it's been reinvented.

This demands an intentional leap from the known into the unknown. It further demands that you live there—in the unknown— for a while. It means discarding the past, everything you once believed to be true.

Think of it as soaring rather than plunging.

Thought Control

You should now be clear about the need to organize your thoughts first, and then your business. Because the organization of your thoughts is the foundation for the organization of your business.

If we try to organize our business without organizing our thoughts, we will fail to attack the problem.

We have seen that organization is not simply time management. Nor is it people management. Nor is it tidying up desks or alphabet-izing patient files. Organization is first, last, and always cleaning up the mess of our minds.

By learning how to *think* about the practice of chiropractic, by learning how to *think* about your priorities, and by learning how to *think* about your life, you'll prepare yourself to do righteous battle with the forces of failure.

Right thinking leads to right action—and now is the time to take action. Because it is only through action that you can translate thoughts into movement in the real world, and, in the process, find fulfillment.

So, first *think* about what you want to do. Then *do* it. Only in this way will you be fulfilled.

How do you put the principles we've discussed in this book to work in your chiropractic practice? To find out, accompany me down the path once more:

1. *Create a story about your practice.* Your story should be an idealized version of your chiropractic practice, a vision of what the preeminent chiropractor in your field should be and why. Your story must become the very heart of your practice. It must become the spirit that mobilizes it, as well as everyone who walks through the doors. Without this story, your practice will be reduced to plain work.

2. *Organize your practice so that it breathes life into your story.* Unless your practice can faithfully replicate your story in action, it all becomes fiction. In that case, you'd be better off not telling your story at all. And without a story, you'd be better off leaving your practice the way it is and just hoping for the best.

Here are some tips for organizing your chiropractic practice:

- Identify the key functions of your practice.
- Identify the essential processes that link those functions.
- Identify the results you have determined your practice will produce.
- Clearly state in writing how each phase will work.

Take it step by step. Think of your practice as a program, a piece of software, a system. It is a collaboration, a collection of processes dynamically interacting with one another.

Of course, your practice is also people.

3. *Engage your people in the process.* Why is this the third step rather than the first? Because, contrary to the advice most business experts will give you, you must never engage your people in the process until you yourself are clear about what you intend to do.

The need for consensus is a disease of today's addled mind. It's a product of our troubled and confused times. When people don't know what to believe in, they often ask others to tell them. To ask is not to lead but to follow.

The prerequisite of sound leadership is first to know where you wish to go.

And so, "What do I want?" becomes the first question; not, "What do they want?" In your own practice, the vision must first be yours. To follow another's vision is to abdicate your personal accountability, your leadership role, your true power.

In short, the role of leader cannot be delegated or shared. And without leadership, no chiropractic practice will ever succeed.

Despite what you have been told, win-win is a secondary step, not a primary one. The opposite of win-win is not necessarily they lose.

Let's say "they" can win by choosing a good horse. The best choice will not be made by consensus. "Guys, what horse do you think we should ride?" will always lead to endless and worthless discussions. By the time you're done jawing, the horse will have already left the post.

Before you talk to your people about what you intend to do in your practice and why you intend to do it, you need to reach agreement with yourself.

It's important to know (1) exactly what you want, (2) how you intend to proceed, (3) what's important to you and what isn't, and (4) what you want the practice to be and how you want it to get there.

Once you have that agreement, it's critical that you engage your people in a discussion about what you intend to do and why. Be clear—both with yourself and with them.

The Story

The story is paramount because it is your vision. Tell it with passion and conviction. Tell it with precision. Never hurry a great story. Unveil it slowly. Don't mumble or show embarrassment. Never apologize or display false modesty. Look your audience in the eyes and tell your story as though it is the most important one they'll ever hear about business. Your business. The business into which you intend to pour your heart, your soul, your intelligence, your imagination, your time, your money, and your sweaty persistence.

Get into the storytelling zone. Behave as though it means everything to you. Show no equivocation when telling your story.

These tips are important because you're going to tell your story over and over—to patients, to new and old employees, to chiropractors, to associate chiropractors, and to your family and friends. You're going to tell it at your church or synagogue, to your card-playing or fishing buddies, and to organizations such as Kiwanis, Rotary, YMCA, Hadassah, and Boy Scouts.

There are few moments in your life when telling a great story about a great business is inappropriate.

If it is to be persuasive, you must love your story. Do you think Walt Disney loved his Disneyland story? Or Ray Kroc his McDonald's story? What about Dave Smith at Federal Express? Or Debbie Fields at Mrs. Field's Cookies? Or Tom Watson Jr. at IBM?

Do you think these people loved their stories? Do you think others loved (and *still* love) to hear them? I daresay *all* successful entrepreneurs have loved the story of their business. Because that's what true entrepreneurs do. They tell stories that come to life in the form of their business.

Remember: A great story never fails. A great story is always a joy to hear.

In summary, you first need to clarify, both for yourself and for your people, the *story* of your practice. Then you need to detail the *process* your practice must go through to make your story become reality.

I call this the business development process. Others call it reengineering, continuous improvement, reinventing your practice, or total quality management.

Whatever you call it, you must take three distinct steps to succeed:

- *Innovation.* Continue to find better ways of doing what you do.
- *Quantification.* Once that is achieved, quantify the impact of these improvements on your practice.
- *Orchestration.* Once these improvements are verified, orchestrate this better way of running your practice so that it becomes your standard, to be repeated time and again.

In this way, the system works—no matter who's using it. And you've built a practice that works consistently, predictably, systematically. A practice you can depend on to operate exactly as promised, every single time.

Your vision, your people, your process—all linked.

A superior chiropractic practice is a creation of your imagination, a product of your mind. So fire it up and get started! Now let's listen to what Dr. Frank has to say about taking action. ✤

CHAPTER 26

Intention without Action Is a Delusion

Dr. Frank Sovinsky

An idea that is developed and put into action is more important than an idea that exists only as an idea.

—The Buddha

Congratulations are in order. Do you realize that only 14 percent of our society will go into a bookstore or library and actually walk out with a book? And only 10 percent of those people will read past the first chapter!

Those who do buy the book intend to read it from cover to cover, and that's where it ends. Intention without action is a delusion! Intention with action is a day well lived.

Now what about you? What are you going to do with this knowledge? Will this book and its ideas just sit on a shelf in your cortex, or will you use it as a platform to launch yourself across the knowing-doing gap?

According to the authors of *The Knowing-Doing Gap*, Jeffrey Pfeffer and Robert I. Sutton, there is a big gap between knowledge of something and translating that knowledge into action. This gap separates the well-meaning, well-intentioned doctor from ever reaching over to the other side. What's on the other side? Your destiny, the life you were born to live.

You already know how to bridge the knowing-doing gap. You have earned the title Doctor of Chiropractic. You worked hard plowing your way through the matriculation process to get a seat at the table. You moved away from friends and family. You made the decision to pursue your dream at any and all costs. You cut off all other career and business possibilities for your life. You took yourself out of the old game to create a new game. You agreed to the financial debt, and you stepped headstrongly into the personal sacrifices.

It took desire, drive, and determination to achieve your degree. You may have wanted to create a better life for you and your family. You might have been moved by a chiropractic experience or the cause of helping people. Regardless of the personal and impersonal reasons, you were determined that nothing would stop you from earning your degree.

You took a risk and you took massive action. Your action paid off; it always does. And here you are.

I have a simple quiz for you. If three frogs are sitting on a lily pad floating in the middle of a pond and one of them decides to jump off, how many frogs are left?

The answer of course is three. Deciding to jump and actually doing it are two separate behaviors.

So there they sit, bobbing up and down and going with the flow. There they sit waiting for the flies to come to them. And for a while there are just enough flies to keep them alive. Yet with each passing day, their vitality slips away. There they sit, wishing for things to be better.

Chiropractors can be just like those frogs sitting on a lily pad. I know because I was one of them. One in three may actually decide to do something about their goals, yet never take any observable action. They treat talking about something as the equivalent to actually doing something.

So there they sit on cushy pad of comfort, floating in a swamp of mediocrity. There they sit, as their practice numbers bob up and down. There they sit, wishing for things to be better.

Fear widens the knowing-doing gap. While fear is your most costly habit, it is cloaked in the behavior we call procrastination. Procrastination is not being lazy. Procrastination is the habit of postponing important actions. When faced with the truth that we need to act, we can resist, resent, or respond.

Resistance is futile unless you are a sleepwalker. Yet resentment works because it takes the pressure off. You may resent having to do all the strategic and tactical work that we outlined in chapters 23 and 24.

So there you sit. You might even feel that you are being singled out for the tough work and that most successful doctors don't have to work on their business. Even if that were true—and it's not—so what?

We are talking to you and about your drive, desire, and determination to get this work done. Keep your eyes on your own paper.

As Michael said, sometimes we take action because we don't want to do something anymore. He said all you have to do is say, "I don't want to do it that way anymore." I followed that advice, and because we are short on time, I will share my top five "I don't want to's."

"I don't want to write reports on weekends."

"I don't want to wait for an insurance company to pay my patients' bill only to have it cut."

"I don't want to stand at a booth at a health fair doing spinal screenings."

"I don't want to worry about money ever again."

"I don't want to have to put up with my employees' attitudes."

Okay, now it's your turn.

"I don't want to . . . "

Sometimes this is where you have to start. When we talk about "practice liberation," we mean it. When you take action and set these systems in motion, your practice works! It's not only freeing you from the mundaneness of doing it all yourself, it sets your mind free from the thoughts of having to do it.

Do, Have, Be

Sometimes we don't take action because we are myth-informed. The myth I am referring to is the "be, do, have" secret to success. If you haven't heard of it, good for you; it's just one less thing to unlearn. I have discovered a more pragmatic order. *Do* something, *have* results, and then *be* better.

Think about it. How can you *be* happy when you are struggling month to month? How can you *be* fulfilled if you haven't even come close to touching as many lives as you intended?

To be or not to be, there is no question. If all you do is sit like a flower (lotus position), being content, waiting to be moved by a mystical moment, then all you will become is blissed out of options.

We only experience our possibilities through our actions. We can only clean up that mess between our ears by experiencing a result of our actions. Whether the result was as intended or not, we can learn. Success and failure both serve as feedback. We innovate (take action), quantify (have a result), and then orchestrate.

The E-Myth call to action includes preparing you and your business for growth simultaneously. This is a big distinction. It's not either/or, it's both. We have shown you areas to focus your attention and how to get to work on your practice. At the same time we have asked probing questions to pique your interest in personal growth as well as professional development.

You have statistics, benchmarks, and accounting instruments to help you see where your practice is, and I suggest you acquire an accurate accounting and appraisal of your personal strengths.

Most people, when asked to describe their talents, have difficulty describing them. Everyone has a unique set of strengths in four areas: emotional intelligence, personal skills, values (motivators), and behavioral traits. Understanding those strengths and leveraging them will minimize the effect of your weaker traits. To learn more about these assessments and personal inventories, go to www.michaelegerber.com/co-author.

A-C-T-I-O-N

You need to build a bridge consisting of six girders to stretch across the knowing-doing gap. If we look at each letter in the word *action* we can see the six girders. They are: Assess, Commit, Target, Influence, Observe, and Now.

A—Assess what needs to be done and then prioritize it. The generic "to do list" does not have the visceral sense of urgency or commitment necessary to make any significant strides. Make a "will do list." Put the day's highest priority at the top and list the rest in order of their urgency. Then determine who will be responsible for the items on the list (accountability). Is it you, your entire team, or one member of your team?

Warning: Many people get so caught up in planning that they just stay there. It's a classic case of "analysis paralysis." They analyze where they are now, where they want to be, and all the options for getting there. All necessary and valuable things, but now is the time for action. Planning for the future isn't enough to produce that future.

C—Commit fully. There is no turning back, so stop looking back. The following quote by Goethe says it best:

"Until one is committed, there is hesitancy, the chance to draw back, always ineffectiveness. Concerning all acts of initiative and creation, there is one elementary truth the ignorance of which kills countless ideas and splendid plans: that the moment one definitely commits oneself, then providence moves too. All sorts of things occur to help one that would never otherwise have occurred. A whole stream of events issues from the decision, raising in one's favor all manner of unforeseen incidents, meetings, and material assistance which no man could have dreamed would have come his way. Whatever you can do or dream you can, begin it. Boldness has genius, power, and magic in it. Begin it now."

T—Target an area where you expect to get short-term results. Set your sights on something that is within reach, not out of sight. For example, doubling a practice from 10 patients a day to 20 day is within reach, while taking a practice of 80 a week to 150 a week in 90 days is out of sight.

I—Influence every stakeholder you have by telling the story of your practice. Inspire your family, your team, your patients, your vendors, and your professional alliances.

Did you know that the word inspiration literally means to "breathe life into"? Can you imagine what it will be like when you breathe life into your practice, your staff, and your patients by telling your practice's story?

You need your people's emotional commitment if your practice is to succeed. Oral commitments—agreeing to do the work—and physical agreements—showing up every workday—are not enough to get the kind of results you are looking for.

O—Observe means that if I were to watch, I could see the action you are taking. It's not just in your head.

If Michael and I were to come to your practice tomorrow, what would we see? Aside from the clinical activities, what would we see as evidence that you are taking action?

Action is measurable and observable. It might be new staff uniforms with name badges or reupholstered tables. It may be a change in a statistic as it closes in on a benchmark. You might even hear someone ask you, "What's gotten into you?" Signs, signs— somewhere there needs to be signs.

N—Now! No excuses, whining, no complaining, just action, now.

Kick the door to that cell wide open, the cell where you have been held captive as a POW, a prisoner of waiting:

- Waiting for kids to get out of school.
- Waiting to start a family.
- Waiting until after vacation.
- Waiting until after the new year, next month, or Monday morning.
- Waiting until they have more time.
- Waiting to get all of your ducks in a row.

Chiropractors who successfully turn knowledge into action have an urgency to do so.

I read a story about Steve Mariucci, former head coach of the San Francisco 49ers. He said that in order to combat the problem he and his team were having, talking more about what needed to be done than actually implementing and doing it, he never wears a watch because "I always know what time it is. It is always *now*. And *now* is when you should do it."

The Story of Your Practice

While touring the walled city of Salzburg, Austria, the birthplace of Wolfgang Amadeus Mozart, I had an "aha" moment. Our guide was telling us about the history and political significance of a particular cathedral. And as she talked, out of the corner of my eye, I saw a marble hand projecting out of the front archway. The hand was worn smooth and looked as if it had been polished. I asked her to explain it.

She told us that this was the symbol for the practice of sanctuary. It meant that a fugitive from the law, enemy of the kingdom, or spiritual outcast could touch the hand, walk into the church and be safe from persecution. The hand had been polished as a result of being touched by hundreds of thousands of pilgrims and tourists.

I did what you would have done. I touched it and entered sanctuary. I felt as if I were entering a place of a higher aim and a higher order.

When you tell the story of your practice, make sure it conveys the feeling of a higher aim. Don't make it about all the clinical services you provide or tether it with chiro-speak. Tell us about sanctuary. Inspire us. Make us believe you mean it.

Is your practice a place where people are accepted as they are? Is your practice a place where they can come for hope and be given a plan? Is it place of a higher order and a place of possibilities?

We always move toward our most dominant thoughts. Write the story of your practice and let it be your most dominant thought.

Imagine the possibilities when the story of your practice is passed from one patient to the next, and on and on.

You are not the sum of your accomplishments or failures. You are not the very worst or the very best thing you have ever done. You are your dreams and the actions you take toward achieving them. In many ways, your actions define who you are.

And one last thing, I hope that someday you'll take the lead from my wife, Cathy, and give this book and a ribbon with a pacifier hanging from it to another chiropractor and say, "Go fix your family's business." It changed my life, and I know you can change that person's. ❖

AFTERWORD

Michael E. Gerber

For more than three decades, I've applied the E-Myth principles I've shared with you here to the successful development of thousands of small businesses throughout the world. Many have been chiropractic practices—from small companies to large corporations, with chiropractors specializing in every field from wellness care to straight chiropractic.

Few rewards are greater than seeing these E-Myth principles improve the work and lives of so many people. Those rewards include seeing these changes:

- Lack of clarity—clarified.
- Lack of organization—organized.
- Lack of direction—shaped into a path that is clearly, lovingly, passionately pursued.
- Lack of money or money poorly managed—money understood instead of coveted; created instead of chased; wisely spent or invested instead of squandered.
- Lack of committed people—transformed into a cohesive community working in harmony toward a common goal; discovering one another and themselves in the process; all the while expanding their understanding, their know-how, their interest, their attention.

After working with so many chiropractors, I know that a practice can be much more than what most become. I also know that nothing is preventing you from making your practice all that it can be. It takes only desire and the perseverance to see it through.

In this book—the next of its kind in the E-Myth Expert series—the E-Myth principles have been complemented and enriched by stories from real-life chiropractors, such as Dr. Frank, who have put these principles to use in their practice. These chiropractors have had the desire and perseverance to achieve success beyond their wildest dreams. Now you, too, can join their ranks.

I hope this book has helped you clear your vision and set your sights on a very bright future.

To your practice and your life, good growing!

ABOUT THE AUTHORS

Michael E. Gerber

Michael E. Gerber is the legend behind the E-Myth series of books, which includes *The E-Myth Revisited*, *E-Myth Mastery*, *The E-Myth Manager*, *The E-Myth Enterprise*, and *Awakening the Entrepreneur Within*. Collectively, his books have sold millions of copies worldwide. He is the founder of In the Dreaming Room™, a 2½-day process to awaken the entrepreneur within, and Origination, which trains facilitators to assist entrepreneurs in growing "turnkey" businesses. He is chairman of the Michael E. Gerber Companies. A highly sought-after speaker and consultant, he has trained hundreds of thousands of business owners in his career. Michael lives with his wife, Luz Delia, in Carlsbad, California.

ABOUT THE AUTHORS

Dr. Frank R. Sovinsky

D r. Frank R. Sovinsky, DC, is a co-founder and CEO of DC Mentors, a client-centered practice management company dedicated to transforming the way chiropractors grow their practices. His passion and genius for understanding human behavior and motivation combined with his pragmatic approach to the business of chiropractic are the reasons his clients are thriving.

Dr. Sovinky's company operates with the E-Myth systems as its foundation. Without them, Dr. Sovinsky would still be living the "Entrepreneurial Myth" as a chiropractor, instead of being free to pursue his dreams. He lives with his wife, Cathy, in Tahoe City, California.

ABOUT THE SERIES

The E-Myth Expert series brings Michael E. Gerber's proven E-Myth philosophy to a wide variety of different professional practice areas. The E-Myth, short for "Entrepreneurial Myth," is simple: too many small businesses fail to grow because their leaders think like technicians, not entrepreneurs. Gerber's approach gives small enterprise leaders practical, proven methods that have already helped transform hundreds of thousands of businesses. Let the E-Myth Expert series boost your professional practice today!

Books in the series include:
The E-Myth Attorney
The E-Myth Accountant
The E-Myth Optometrist
The E-Myth Chiropractor
The E-Myth Financial Advisor

Forthcoming books in the series include:
The E-Myth Landscape Contractor
The E-Myth Architect
The E-Myth Real Estate Brokerage
The E-Myth Real Estate Investor
The E-Myth Insurance Store
… and 300 more industries and professions

Learn more at: www.michaelegerber.com/co-author

Have you created an E-Myth enterprise? Would you like to become a co-author of an E-Myth book in your industry? Go to www.michaelegerber.com/co-author.

THE MICHAEL E. GERBER
ENTREPRENEUR'S LIBRARY
It Keeps Growing...

Thank you for reading another E-Myth Vertical book.

Who do you know who is an expert in their industry?

Who has applied The E-Myth to the improvement of their
practice as Dr. Frank Sovinsky has?

Who can add immense value to others in his or her industry
by sharing what he or she has learned?

Please share this book with that individual and share that individual with us.

We at Michael E. Gerber Companies are determined to transform the state
of small business and entrepreneurship worldwide. *You can help.*

To find out more, email us at Michael E. Gerber Partners, at
gerber@michaelegerber.com.

To find out how *YOU* can apply the E-Myth to *YOUR* practice,
contact us at gerber@michaelegerber.com.

Thank you for living your Dream, and changing the world.

Authors of Business Design

Michael E. Gerber, Co-Founder/Chairman
Michael E. Gerber Companies™
Creator of The E-Myth Evolution™
P.O. Box 131195, Carlsbad, CA 92013
760-752-1812 O • 760-752-9926 F
gerber@michaelegerber.com
www.michaelegerber.com

Join The Evolution^{SM}

Find the latest updates:
www.michaelegerber.com

Attend the Dreaming Room Trainings
www.michaelegerber.com

Listen to the Michael E. Gerber Radio Show
www.blogtalkradio.com/michaelegerber

Watch the latest videos
www.youtube.com/michaelegerber

Connect on LinkedIn
www.linkedin.com/in/michaelegerber

Connect on Facebook
www.facebook.com/MichaelEGerberCo

Follow on Twitter
http://twitter.com/michaelegerber

CPSIA information can be obtained at www.ICGtesting.com
Printed in the USA
LVOW061013130112

263649LV00001B/1/P